Love Our Cities

"This is the book transformational city leaders have been waiting for. Love Our Cities is the playbook to begin your transformational journey into your city. A "Love Your City" event will act as a first domino that changes the relationship between the church and others who love your city. Author Jeff Pishney takes you into "the room where it happens" to share his journey that began with one church in Modesto to now include hundreds of churches in scores of cities around the nation. The case studies and testimonials ("City Spotlights") alone, at the end of each chapter, are worth the price of the book. This is a movement that wants to happen...that is waiting to happen in your city. Pull out your high-lighter and get ready to be challenged and get ready to act."

Eric Swanson
Senior Fellow at Leadership Network
Co-author of *The Externally Focused Church*,
To Transform a City and others

"I talk and write about the idea of falling in love with place and the value that brings to both the residents and the community as a whole. This fine book is a lived example of that love. There is no playbook for love, but there is the experience that Jeff and his collaborators in Modesto have shared. From that city and many more we can take lessons and inspiration to make our own cities, our own neighborhoods, better, more interesting, more lovable places."

Peter Kageyama
Author, *For the Love of Cities*
Senior Fellow, The Alliance for Innovation

"In a world awash in bad news, *Love Our Cities* glows with life and hope. In a world pulling apart, Love Our Cities shows how communities can pull together and how simple acts of Christian service can still build bridges. This is no book of wishful thinking or pie-in-the-sky dreams, but rather a hands-on field guide for the what, why and how of loving a city well. I've seen Jeff in action and experienced LOC firsthand in my hometown: this is where love's rubber meets our cities' roads."

Jedd Medefind
President, Christian Alliance for Orphans

"The events of the past few years have created division in our cities as most have not seen in their lifetimes. Division seems to almost be natural, but unity is hard. City pride is even harder to advance today. Doing good things together can be the push toward what is good in a city and this Jeff and Eric provide what you need to get started. Once hope and unity are in motion, steady and persistent activity can keep it going indefinitely. Flourishing begins with action that produces positive results - that brings love to those in the city. *Love Our Cities* describes the propellant that cities need to begin and gives a playbook so that hope can be seem and division can be eliminated. If you want to gather those who desire to serve, cause great impact to be experienced, and accelerate unity that will transform where you live, this is the book you need."

Jim Liske

Founder and Principle, 1 26a Coaching and Consulting

"Love Modesto transformed our city! Jeff Pishney's vision of love, compassion and service was sincerely communicated from day one. He created something everyone wanted to be a part of. I'm grateful for him and our community's continued desire to Love Modesto!"

Sue Zwahlen

Mayor of Modesto, California

"*Love Our Cities* is the real deal. I have known Jeff Pishney for over a decade and have learned a lot from being around him and Love Our Cities. He is both a thought leader and practitioner. This book proves a road map and practical examples of how communities can be transformed for the better. It's a must read for anyone who wants to make an impact in the place where they live!"

Dave Runyon

The Art of Neighboring & CityUnite

"*Love Our Cities* is a living, breathing, story of how our serving impacts the lives and institutions of the cities we live in. Through serving, people learn to love their cities. Through serving love becomes an action verb that plants its roots deep within us. This book is grounded in practical advice that builds community as people work together to bring hope. Love Our Cities will change both you and the city where you live for good."

Glenn Barth
President, GoodCities

"Every community has interest in serving, the challenge is harnessing that interest. Love Our Cities delivers a turnkey pathway that mobilizes the latent interest to serve that exists in every community. It's like the Quick Start Guide for collaborative impact. Careful though, with all that interest turned to action, you just might have a city movement on your hands!"

Dave Bushnell
Founder, Mobilize Leadership

"Jeff Pishney and Eric Jung has written a breathtaking book about the ways that God is stirring city by city to see those same cities flourish. We are in a moment in US and global history where faith has to be demonstrated to be believed. This is a powerful apologetic to transform a city through ordinary persons who love God and love their city."

Dr. Mac Pier
Founder, Movement.org

"The *Love Our Cities* story is as wonderful as it is simple. Then most great ideas and movements are. This story is transformational at several levels. First of all, it is personally transformational in that it's a story about lifting our eyes from traditional activities to love and bless cities. Secondly, it is transformational in that it is calling for engagement and collaboration, not only for churches, but also with people of good will across a city, for the sake of the city. This story, if heeded by all, will energize your city with a fresh vision."

Ian Shelton
Coordinator, Movement Australia

L♥ve Our Cities

How a city-wide volunteer day can
unite and transform your community

Jeff Pishney
Eric Jung

NEW YORK

LONDON • NASHVILLE • MELBOURNE • VANCOUVER

L♥ve Our Cities

How a city-wide volunteer day can unite and transform your community

Published in New York, New York, by Morgan James Publishing. Morgan James is a trademark of Morgan James, LLC. www.MorganJamesPublishing.com

All images owned by Love Our Cities or used by permission of affiliate organizations.

Scripture quotations marked NCV are from the The Holy Bible, New Century Version®. Copyright © 2005 by Thomas Nelson, Inc.

Scripture quotations marked The Message (MSG) Copyright © 1993, 2002, 2018 by Eugene H. Peterson

Proudly distributed by Ingram Publisher Services.

Morgan James BOGO™

A **FREE** ebook edition is available for you or a friend with the purchase of this print book.

[_____]

CLEARLY SIGN YOUR NAME ABOVE

Instructions to claim your free ebook edition:
1. Visit MorganJamesBOGO.com
2. Sign your name CLEARLY in the space above
3. Complete the form and submit a photo of this entire page
4. You or your friend can download the ebook to your preferred device

ISBN 9781636980133 paperback
ISBN 9781636980140 ebook
Library of Congress Control Number: 2022943377

Cover and Interior Design by:
Chris Treccani
www.3dogcreative.net

Morgan James PUBLISHING Builds with... **Habitat for Humanity** Peninsula and Greater Williamsburg

Morgan James is a proud partner of Habitat for Humanity Peninsula and Greater Williamsburg. Partners in building since 2006.

Get involved today! Visit MorganJamesPublishing.com/giving-back

To all those who love your city around the world …

not complaining about your city,
putting down your city,
or just talking about how to improve your city,

but the ones who want to do something to see
their city be the best it can be.

This book is for you!

Love Our Cities equips people like you to lead a city-wide volunteer day, a catalytic event that will become a hub for ongoing city-wide initiatives to create lasting change and unity in your city.

Born in Modesto, California in 2009, our first city-wide volunteer day has spread to over 100 cities, more than 225,000 volunteers, and over 1 million volunteer hours totaling more than $28.5 million dollars in service!

Our goal is to help over 1,000 cities around the world in the next 10 years!

Visit us at LoveOurCities.org to learn more about our efforts and how to get your city started.

100% of profits from the sale of this book go to support the ongoing work of Love Our Cities.

Thank you for your support.

Table of Contents

Foreword

"Great minds think alike". Or maybe better, "an idea whose time has come". That's what struck me as I read my friends Jeff Pishney and Eric Jung's new book Love Our Cities. All around the USA I see people and churches of all sorts coming together to make a difference, to seek the peace and prosperity of the places where we live and work. If God really is God, and he loves us and all our cities, if He is inspiring people and churches to be the best witness possible, to impact and change our cities, then why wouldn't we expect that many different places would be on similar journeys? Journeys of discovering the incredible power of unity within a community. The power of working together for the common good, despite our differences.

Here in my home city of Portland Oregon, we've been on our own journey of figuring out what on earth we're here for as a group of people trying to follow the example of Jesus. How do we actually serve our neighbors effectively? How do we overcome the many barriers that so many have? Barriers that keep people from following Jesus. Barriers like feeling that the church is more about what it's against than what it's for. That it's about keeping people down and controlling their natural instincts toward freedom and productivity. That's it's primarily about judging, keeping score, and being afraid of progress. We found ourselves sitting in our city's mayor's office apologizing for not being part of the solution and asking a simple question. "If we could mobilize thousands of our folks to love and serve Portland, what could we do to help?". That was 15 years ago, and now TogetherPDX has been flourishing for all this time. Uniting hundreds of churches and non-profits to beautify the city, care for our children in foster care, improve our public schools, and serve our newly arriving refugees, for starters.

My dad was an evangelist named Luis Palau. He was from Argentina and came to Portland Oregon more than 60 years ago to study at a seminary where he met my mom. Despite decades of traveling the globe sharing the "good news", Portland became home and we all came to love our city. Even though evangelists haven't typically been known for activating the church toward social justice and serving the community, my dad knew that unless people sensed the love that we had for them and for the broader community, our message would fall flat. My dad was there with me when we met the mayor for that first conversation. We were honest. We knew the church in our city had unintentionally become far more known for what we were against than what we were for, perhaps even unfairly. But if we wanted to be part of changing some of these negative stereotypes, we knew it was on us—the people that claimed to be attempting to follow Jesus, however imperfectly. My dad grew to love Portland in a fresh way, even though this journey began after he'd hit his 70's. He became aware of Jeff and the Love Modesto movement because Modesto was the place where he'd done his first ever unified outreach in the United States—way back in 1982. I was a student at Wheaton College at the time, and I still remember him expressing his excitement about that event. Love Modesto's approach adds a unique layer to the journey many of us, like my dad I, have been on.

Some feel a 'one and done' day of volunteerism is perfect to make those serving feel better, but does little to change the underlying conditions in a city. My experience has been the opposite. A well planned and supported experience is often exactly what's needed, it becomes a catalyst, sparking something new ... new vision, new faith to believe things can change and new relationships within and outside of the church community.

Divisions build up (between denominations, ethnicities, socio-economic groups—I could go on, but you get the picture) for many reasons. Some are very deep and require asking for forgiveness for trust to be rebuilt. That's the very reason that a catalytic experience can be just the 'excuse' to set aside our differences to live out our faith together. To focus on 'common good', 'common ground' issues that unite us, instead of focusing on the endless political, social, or theological issues that tend to divide, discourage, and make us woefully ineffective in our efforts to build a better community and city.

These days some people look down on volunteerism as passe, maybe even toxic charity that does more harm than good. I thoroughly disagree. Yes, overeager volunteers that come into a neighborhood without getting to know the residents and without engaging their wisdom and energy can face an uphill battle (see chapter 7!). I'm a firm believer in 'asset-based community development' that starts with a positive look at the beauty and resilience of those living in a community, at what they have rather than what they don't have. As Jeff and Eric explain, we have to start by asking meaningful questions, taking the time to prepare well and work with those who live and know their community and its history. This is especially essential when working across racial and socio-economic divides. It's what I love about this book and the models laid out. Jeff and Eric have taken these hard earned 'best practices' into account. Sometimes the only way to learn is to make lots of mistakes. Better to learn from someone else's mistakes than your own!

You may be a church or community leader longing to see lasting change come to your city or neighborhood. You may be an individual feeling a bit powerless to make a difference in the face of the sometimes overwhelming obstacles facing us. Obstacles such as homelessness, joblessness, a challenged foster care or public school system. The good news is that in city after city there are examples of tangible, sustainable differences being made, building on the love we each have for our cities and the people in our cities. This book is a testimony to the kind of movement one person and one church can start. You can't do it alone, but it is doable. Love Our Cities has proven it time and time again.

A final word. Many of us have been inspired by books and messages that fire us up, that inspire us to dream big about the impact we could make. Far fewer provide the very tangible, actionable, proven and tested steps that can be put into practice. This book includes practical nuts and bolts ideas that can lead you to put on a volunteer day you can be proud of and that can make a lasting difference in many lives. You can build on that to help develop a sustainable movement in your community.

Now is the time to love our cities well. To be willing to join forces with those we agree with and those we may disagree with. After all, we're all here, in this season of time, for a reason. I believe that. I believe God can use you to make your neighborhood and city a better place for everyone. A place where kids and families can flourish and become more of what God intended for all of us. I hope that this book does more than inspire you, I hope it challenges you to take the next step for your city.

Let the adventure begin!
Kevin Palau - CEO, Luis Palau Association

Luis Palau and "Big Red" in 2011

Preface

Hey, this is Jeff, let's get this out of the way up front—I never thought I would write a book or even team up to write one. I did just enough work on papers in college to get by and I was more than happy when that part of life was over. Don't get me wrong, I like books, I like learning new things, but to be perfectly honest I would prefer to be out putting what I am learning into practice. I am a practitioner, not a theorist. I get antsy at conferences that go on too long because I can't put into practice the things I am learning. I was even pacing the room in every meeting we had to make this book happen. Because of all that I can promise this book is *not* going to be overly long or full of fluff. I don't have the time or the patience for it and neither do you.

When we started, I had no idea how much time and effort went into creating a book. Like I said, I am not a writer, so we worked with an old roommate of mine who is a writer to make this happen. He spent a couple of days interviewing Eric and I, honing what we wanted to say and why, created a manuscript from those interviews and then we went through the process of revisions, edits, clarifying statements and a whole lot more. Oh, and we started this thing just before a pandemic and there were job changes and, well, there was a lot.

This is Eric, my story is definitely not Jeff's. I don't do what he does, I am not a former pastor (I do have a seminary degree, though). I was flipping houses when I was 22. I have been and remain in the business world as well as the world of nonprofits. My family moved back to Modesto, California in 2009, when NOBODY was moving to Modesto. Height of the recession, jobs were scarce. This is mostly Jeff's story at the beginning, but his passion was contagious, and I found myself pulled in. You'll hear a bit more about how I come into all this later, but like Jeff I never thought I would be working on a book. It has been an adventure, that's for sure.

If all of that is true, why did we write the book in the first place? Bottom line, this book exists because a lot of people kept telling us that it needed to be written, that the story of Love Modesto and Love Our Cities needed to be told. So here we are. We are telling this story because we believe that it matters. It matters in our city and yours. Love Modesto and Love Our Cities is not really about us, we're just one part of the story. As you read through this book you will see what we mean. And by the way, if COVID and racial tensions, political turmoil and all the rest have shown me anything, it's that what Love Our Cities is all about is *even more* needed today than when we started.

We live in crazy and divisive times. We can see, and feel, that fact every day and everywhere. The truth is that there are lots of people doing lots of great things. In cities around the country there are people quietly doing good work, leading initiatives for schools, homelessness, foster care, anti-trafficking, neighborhoods and the list goes on. What they often don't have is a catalyst to unify those efforts and give a boost to those ongoing efforts. More than anything else, what we do at Love Our Cities provides that link, that boost, a way for a champion to stand up for their city.

Our city-wide volunteer days make a real difference. They bring every-one together--no one divides over volunteerism or making their city a bet-ter place to live. Not so long ago at one of our events I saw 2 people work-ing side by side at a local nonprofit. One was wearing a t-shirt supporting one presidential candidate. The other, you guessed it, wearing a t-shirt for the other candidate. And they were getting along, doing something good for our city. I saw adults and kids of all backgrounds working together to beautify a local park. In these difficult times it is more important than ever to work together in love, to better the cities that we call home. We believe it matters and we have seen it makes a real difference firsthand.

It's our hope that our story will be a catalyst for you. Maybe you need to change your thinking, maybe you just need a push. I (Jeff) certainly didn't expect this thing that captured my heart and mind to become what it is, but I am so glad that it did.

Here's another thing you need to know up front: Love Modesto started in and through a church where I was on staff as a pastor, Love Our Cities soon grew out of that. That means there is definitely a "faith component" to what this is all about. In fact, it's really what drives my heart for people. It also means that you're going to hear some faith language and Bible references throughout this book. I'm not apologizing for it, because it really does shape who I am. At the same time, I am not going to beat you over the head with it nor am I trying to alienate anyone who doesn't share a Christian faith. If you have a different faith or none at all, we want you on board with what we're doing. Chances are you may find some of the things a bit strange or uncomfortable. I just ask that you hear us out. Give us a chance and test what we're saying. If we don't measure up, that's on us. If you just can't get on board, ok, but at least you'll understand.

To all the church leaders I hope read this book: I am one of you. I mean that. I spent 20 years on staff as a pastor. I can do the secret handshake, but I'm not going to because this book is about a story that is bigger than any one church. You are going to read things in this book that may make you uncomfortable. Yes, there's Bible language, but probably not as much as you might expect. That's on purpose. We're asking you to look past your normal boundaries, to come alongside people who you don't agree with and work together for the common good, the good of our cities—loving them like Jesus does!

Jeff Pishney, CEO and Founder Love Modesto and Love Our Cities
Eric Jung, Director of Policy, Titan Solar Power and Love Our Cities Board Member

Introduction

It's 8:45am, the sun inches its way over the roof of our city's event center. From the stage, I feel the shadows fade as we come into the light. I look out over two city blocks and see a crowd of over 5,000 people. On my left at the end of the block, sunlight fills a 40-foot American flag hanging from a fire truck ladder. As my gaze moves to the right, I notice the 40 vendors lining the outer edges of the streets. As I look down to my right and I see our city's mayor and our county's CEO chatting with some of our event sponsors. I close my eyes for a moment soaking in Journey's "Don't Stop Believin'" blaring from the speakers on each side of me.

As I open my eyes, our Emcees are next to me playing the air guitar and T-shirt cannons are firing Love Modesto gear into the crowd. I see smiling faces, young and old, every ethnicity and background that makes up our city. I see church leaders and my friend the Imam. I see the rabbi and my atheist neighbor too. I see Spider-Man... Wait, did I just see Spider-Man? And I realize, this isn't just a crowd, these are my neighbors. Sure, we have our differences, but we all care about this place we call home. We love Modesto!

Just for a moment, I think back to when this journey began in 2009. Our city was considered one of the worst cities in America. I was the outreach pastor at a local church, trying to figure out how to make an impact in our city and hoping to get 100 people from our church to show up for a volunteer day. Now we're throwing the largest block party in our city (on a Saturday morning)! All I can think is, "God, never in my wildest dreams could I have imagined this."

By 1 o'clock that afternoon, over 7,250 people had volunteered on over 100 projects, providing nearly a million dollars in community service to our city (according to independentsector.org). We cleaned up parks and downtown. Crews went to work at over 30 schools. We sent people out to welcome refugees and encourage seniors at assisted living homes. Clothes were donated to people in need. People helped out at animal shelters. Others learned about sex trafficking and what they could do to help. We had a blood drive and helped the Salvation Army, cleaned up the river and the streets, assisted Meals on Wheels, helped in hospitals, and I could go on. Churches and insurance companies, the local health club, doctors and accounting firms, plumbers and car dealerships, business and nonprofits all came together as sponsors. Our last count had over 400 businesses, organizations and congregations coming together to Love Modesto on one day.

I get excited just thinking back on it. Without a doubt though, as I think about all that was done here in my hometown, one of my favorite parts of the day was being able to help one of our over 100 city partners, Love Paradise, as they began to recover from the deadliest wildfire in California history. Paradise is a community a couple of hours north of us. That fire wiped out 90% of their community. Shortly after the last flames were extinguished, we asked our Love Paradise leader, a high school teacher, how we could tangibly help his community. He said his city needed hope and something to rally around, something that they could wear with pride as a reminder of what tied them together. He asked for white t-shirts with the "Love Paradise" logos on the front just like our Love Modesto shirts. We were able to raise enough money to send over 1,700 shirts to their community as a show of support and solidarity. It was a small gesture, but it was a shot in the arm of hope and commonality when they needed it most. Seeing our city banding together to help not only ourselves but others as well gets to the heart of why we exist.

This is Jeff, CEO and Founder of Love Modesto and Love Our Cities, (more on how that works in a minute), and I could spend all day talking about my city. I can talk your ears off about its history, its people and yes, its challenges. The city-wide volunteer day we do every April is a whole lot of fun (and I'm not gonna lie—a whole lot of work to pull off!). It's a great party, but it's only a part of what we do. And what we do is a whole lot bigger than just Modesto, California. Eric Jung (one of our founding board members and co-author) and I, hope that's where you will come into this story.

How We Got Here

What started in Modesto (just over 12 years ago as I write this), has now spread to over 100 active cities across the nation (and we have talked with a lot more than that). The very first Love Modesto event happened on March 7, 2009. It started at Big Valley Grace Community Church, where I was on staff as a pastor. It didn't take long for it to take on a life of its own, a life so big that it would lead me to leave my job at the church in order to begin and lead a nonprofit organization dedicated to helping cities across the nation start similar movements. Love Our Cities has become the umbrella for a nationwide phenomenon. Love Modesto was the start, but it didn't take too long before other cities saw what we were doing and soon Love Fullerton, Colorado Springs and Albuquerque and Hartford and Green Bay and . . .well you get the idea. Our goal is simple: to love our cities so that our cities will thrive. In 2019 alone, over 45,000 people volunteered with Love Our Cities, but that doesn't begin to tell the story. At the time I am writing this, over 100 cities and 225,000 people nationwide have volunteered their time because they love their cities, since 2009. Based on our research, that means over 1,000,000 volunteer hours and $28.5 million in service completed.

Today, Modesto, California is in better shape than it was when we first started in 2009. Then the city was in really rough shape. Today we see a spirit of beautiful collaboration between the various groups in our town (we call them sectors). Churches and nonprofits, local and county government, schools and businesses have come together in ways that a decade ago would have seemed unthinkable. Love Modesto has become the bridge to community engagement for all of those sectors. We are looked to as the group who brings people from a variety of backgrounds together to get things done for our city. But it wasn't always that way.

But I am getting ahead of myself.

First things first. Why are you here? Why are you reading this book? If I had to guess, whether you are a church leader, work for a nonprofit or local government, or are "just" a person who looks at your city, you're finding yourself saying "Something has got to change, we're broken, and I can't sit by anymore." Chances are you are saying it a lot. And you are not alone.

The stats say that over most of the last 40 years, somewhere in the neighborhood of two-thirds to three-fourths of Americans believe that our nation is headed in the wrong direction.[1] As Eric says: "If we are unhappy with the narrative of our nation, at the end of the day, we have got to recognize that we as its citizens have to recognize that we are the narrators. And if we are upset with the narrative then we really have to start thinking about what our role is in changing that narrative."[2]

I believe that.

All across the nation people like you and people like me are looking for ways to, as one author I read a long time ago said, "give up our hack dreams of trying to 'make a difference in the world' and start dreaming God-sized dreams of making the world different."[3] We believe in working for the common good of our cities. We have joined hundreds of thousands of people who do too. Together we have made our cities just a bit better.

If this resonates with you, we think you'll enjoy this book, and we hope that it will inspire you to take the next step. This isn't meant to be a hard sell. This isn't about pitching a program that can solve all of your city's problems. At its core this is a story about how an event helped bring people together and provide hope, and it's about how others have taken that model and found similar results in their own communities. Yes, we are passionate about this, because we have seen it work here in Modesto and all around the country. If nothing else, it should bring you hope as to what is possible when people come together.

---

1   Dean Obeidallah, "We've Been on the Wrong Track Since 1972," Daily Beast, https://www.thedailybeast.com/weve-been-on-the-wrong-track-since-1972 (accessed 9/26/2019)
2   See Eric's Tedx Talk which can be found at www.loveourcities.org/tedtalk.
3   Leonard I. Sweet, *Soul Tsunami* (Grand Rapids: Zondervan, 1999), 16.

If you are at all like us, you are looking for something that you can actually do, something that will help your community to actually change. Maybe you are just dipping your toe in the water of community engagement (maybe you don't even know what "community engagement" looks like or means). Maybe you have started an initiative in your community and are looking for a way to build momentum. No matter whether you are just starting to explore the possibilities or whether you have been at this for a long time, Love Our Cities wants to help. We operate from a simple idea: come alongside people like you so that you can come alongside people in your community to make things better. We believe that a city-wide volunteer day like the one I just told you about will provide more benefits to your city than you can imagine. This book addresses the method behind the madness, why it works, and the practical next steps that you can take to start a city-wide volunteer day.

We aren't offering a one-size-fits-all cookie cutter sort of approach. Instead, we want to show you principles that can easily be adapted to the needs of your city. Think of Modesto and some of the other cities that you are going to read about as the lab that proved the ideas and practices that have made Love Our Cities uniquely successful. Love Our Cities has helped cities all over the country to do something unique. Our city-wide volunteer day has become the catalyst to connect ongoing initiatives, build networks and help grow a community buy-in for programs and organizations already on the ground in a way that rarely happens. It's not that there are no other volunteer days out there. We've seen lots—city government events, events from one or even several cooperating churches, but none that we know of (and many leaders across the world have confirmed this) that bring the whole community together like we've been able to do.

In order to keep things simple, short and as practical as possible, we have broken the book into four parts. Part One explains how we got from Love Modesto in 2009 to over 100 cities that are a part of our Love Our Cities network in 2020. Part Two looks at some of the elements we believe are necessary to understand before doing any community engagement. Together these elements create a solid foundation for long-term success. Part Three gets really practical, looking at the nuts and bolts of running a city-wide volunteer day. Part Four takes everything to the next level, showing you how a successful city-wide volunteer day has changed the game, and helps you think about what a year-round city movement might look like. (If you are wondering about how to pay for all of this, don't worry, chapter 12 dives into funding channels).

Along the way, we shine a spotlight on cities that have partnered with us, cities where the principles that you are reading about in this book are being worked out. Love Our Cities is not just a Modesto, California thing, it works across the country from California to New Mexico, Colorado to Washington, South Carolina to Connecticut. We know these stories will encourage and inspire you to dream about what can happen in your city, which is why the very last city spotlight is blank. It's yours to write. Because after all, we know that you love your city as much as we love Modesto, and we can't wait to hear all about it.

Let's dive in.

Part 1:

Responding to the Needs of Our Cities

Hey, this is Eric.

National polls confirm most of us believe our country is headed in the wrong direction and has been doing so for over 40 years. Would you like to guess the period when we had the highest approval rating? The four months after 9/11.

What?

How does that make sense? I don't even have to put a full date, and everyone knows what I am talking about. I am typing these words 19 years and 15 days after the event, and it still hits me. Arguably the worst national tragedy of my lifetime. And yet in the aftermath of that event, that horrible, gut-wrenching event, something amazing happened. People pulled together, an entire country pulled together, if only for a moment. The thing is, this is not entirely unknown. Sebastian Junger recounts the following story:

> The one thing that might be said for societal collapse is that—for a while at least—everyone is equal. In 1915 an earthquake killed 30,000 people in Avezzano, Italy, in less than a minute. The worst-

hit areas had a mortality rate of 96 percent. The rich were killed along with the poor. Virtually everyone who survived was immediately thrust into the most basic struggle for survival: they needed food, they needed water, they needed shelter, and they needed to rescue the living and bury the dead. … "An earthquake achieves what the law promises but does not in fact maintain," one of the survivors wrote. "The equality of all men."[4]

There is something about tragedy that tends to bring people together, at least for a moment of time. Junger shows that this is true in multiple times and places, including, notably, in London during the blitz in World War II. Look around, pick a city big or small and the word "crisis" doesn't seem altogether inappropriate, does it? I don't have to point you to the headlines for you to know that this is true. New York, Chicago, LA, San Francisco. Murder, homelessness, violent crime, gangs, drugs, the list could go on. That's just the "big" cities. What about the smaller ones? Opioid crisis, unemployment, illiteracy, poverty. What about your city?

But for all their problems, we love our cities. We love where we're from, even if there are things that drive us nuts about them. Over our years doing this we have found the vast majority of people love where they are from, where they live, and they want it to be better.

Our cities bring us together. I don't mean roads or parks or monuments or buildings or restaurants or sports teams, even though those are the things that we often think about when we imagine our city. The root word in Latin for cities means citizens. Place is important, don't get me wrong, but why do those places matter? Because of what happens there and who it happens with. So, when we talk about loving our cities and improving where we live, we are really talking about loving the people who make up our communities. The real question is, do we actually care? The needs are great.

Someone has to do something.

---

4   Sebastian Junger, *Tribe: On Homecoming and Belonging*, (New York: Twelve, 2016), 43-44.

Why not me? Why not us?

What can I do? How can I change the narrative of my city? What can you do? The next three chapters walk you through what happened to Jeff and our city of Modesto, where all of it led as he, and later I and a bunch of others, tried to help figure those questions out. As you read these chapters, think about your city and what you can be doing to respond to the needs of the people there.

One thing you should know about Jeff is he's an activator. He's the get in there and get it done guy. He's uber-relational and can make a lot of things happen. It's impressive and inspiring, but it can also be intimidating. A lot of us, even those of us who are on the same page with someone like that, who want to see their vision happen, can get overwhelmed. We can easily get knocked back and think "there's no way that I can do that, I'm not like that." Don't worry, we are very aware that there are only a few Jeff's in the world, and we don't think you have to be him in order to help your city. I'm not. We have worked with leaders across the country who have very different personalities and skill sets, most of them are not like Jeff at all and they are thriving as they help their cities.

Buckle up, it has been quite a ride, and we think that you will be encouraged and inspired.

Modesto Sucks!

"In doing something, do it with LOVE or never do it at all."
— Mahatma Gandhi

Jeff's Story

"**M**odesto Sucks!"

It's not exactly the kind of statement that you want to have said about your town. The problem was it was on t-shirts worn by a couple of college kids. It was probably somewhere around 2005, and I was the college pastor at Big Valley Grace Community Church.

I am not from Modesto, I moved here in 1995, just out of grad school and never left. It's my city. I chose it. Why should you care about Modesto, California? What does it have to do with life in the Lexington, Kentucky or Wichita, Kansas or Sandusky, Ohio or any of a hundred or thousand other places across the United States (or around the world for that matter)? Several years ago, I was interviewed by a professor from a Japanese university doing research on religion in the US. He told me that in many ways Modesto was almost a prototype for cities across the US. A mix of agriculture and urban center, a broad cross section of ethnic backgrounds and economic statuses. Modesto, it turns out, could be Anywhere, USA.

I grew up in Cedar Rapids, Iowa. Cedar Rapids is a mid-sized city which as odd as it sounds, is not too different from Modesto. Replace cornfields with almond and walnut orchards and factor in much better weather and there are a lot of similarities (for the record, I knew nothing about farming then and I still don't). Modesto is my city. I love Modesto. It's my home. It's not just the history or the places. It's the people. The friendships. My family. So "Modesto Sucks!" hit home for me literally and figuratively. It was a wound in my soul.

To be fair, the college group included hundreds and there may have been two kids that I remember wearing the black "Modesto Sucks!" t-shirts. For the most part, these college kids were pushing me, pushing us as a church, to actually live out our faith.

Really, the genesis of this whole Love Modesto, Love Our Cities thing really started with that college group I led for 9 years. The college young people wanted to do church differently. These young people, college kids, were idealists. They wanted to see their faith relevant and lived out, they wanted more than just sitting down in a chair every Sunday listening to a sermon. It was really them pushing us to do things out in the community. I remember one Thanksgiving going with a bunch of them to a mobile home park to help serve meals to people, rather than spending the morning on parades or football or whatever. We did family stuff later in the day, but for at least the morning we got our attention off ourselves and focused on others in our community. In 9 years, we did a whole heck of a lot of stuff in our community.

I didn't know it then, but I was being set up. God was working on me, shaping me through these kids and the people we interacted with. He was shaping me through my wife, through other leaders, through the books I was reading. All of that stuff was working on my heart, on the way that I thought about people and what it really meant to live in the way of Jesus.

In 2007, my role on church staff changed to be the outreach pastor. They wanted me to take a lot of those same things that we did in the college group to the rest of the big church, because while the rest of the church was really good at financially supporting organizations that were doing great things, we needed to grow in volunteering and engaging in our community. Our church leaders saw what we're doing in the college group and said, "Can you bring some of that to the rest of the church?" I think that was a major reason why they hired me.

As a church, we were asking a lot of really good questions in 2007. Questions that started us on a trajectory toward what would become Love Modesto and later Love Our Cities. What did it mean to love God and love our neighbors? I was asking a lot of those questions. I often felt like I was being hammered over and over again. "Jeff, what are you doing?", but I often lacked clarity on how to properly respond... then the Great Recession hit.

It's an understatement to say that the Great Recession of 2008 was not kind to Modesto. Housing tanked and foreclosures were everywhere, the economy was awful. Crime was up. We hit "worst places to live" lists. High unemployment. Things weren't going well. You could practically see the city crumbling around us. Prospects didn't look great. The message of those t-shirts was like a festering sore in my heart and mind. I hated it. It also seemed strangely prophetic because in 2008 it really did suck in Modesto.

In some ways, Modesto's 2008 reality was not so different from its past. Started in 1870, Modesto was the epitome of an Old West railroad town. It's almost a cliché: saloons, cowboys, prostitution, opium dens, gambling, shootouts in the streets: if there was a vice to be found, Modesto had it. Through at least the mid 1880s, it was often a lawless, though prosperous place. The breakneck pace of growth was largely unchecked and without planning. Soon opium dens, gambling houses and red-light districts could be found in the middle of residential and business districts. In 2008 we were bigger, more sophisticated, and many of the problems we faced were centered on the same street that the problems were centered on in the

1870s and 1880s—9ᵗʰ Street. There were systemic issues that were rearing their ugly heads because of the recession.

Local legend has it that the town got its name because San Francisco banker and Central Pacific board member William Ralston was too modest to have it bear his name. Many of the early buildings in Modesto were literally moved from other small towns. One of those towns was Paradise, (no, not the same one that burned), a ferry town that was where the railroad should have gone but they wouldn't play ball with the railroad. So the railroad built Modesto and within a year it was the county seat. Paradise and other surrounding communities were not much more than a memory. There is something more than a little telling in that the birth of Modesto destroyed Paradise.

The construction of the railroad through the San Joaquin Valley brought workers from all over the world. African Americans, Latinos, and Chinese were all early settlers though not always welcomed by the white settlers. During the 1870s, even as the railroad crews moved north, connecting Sacramento to Los Angeles, Modesto prospered due to wheat crops. The town was so lawless and the legal system so overwhelmed, that in the late 1870's a vigilante group—the San Joaquin Regulators—decided that enough was enough. Hooded, the regulators "invited" undesirables to leave town at gunpoint. At least one was killed. But the regulators didn't just target criminals—anyone deemed undesirable was at risk. African Americans, Latinos and especially the Chinese were targeted and blamed for Modesto's crime problem. African American settlers tended to live outside of town on the west side, Latinos largely on the southwest side.

In the intervening years Modesto has had its share of ups and downs. Things got better and worse. Recessions and resurgences. Emphasis on education and music. Fires and rebuilding. Through it all, the underbelly was there, never too far away. In the early 1900s there was a huge problem with alcoholism and morphine addiction. Saloons continued to outnumber churches. The town has continued to grow. The Gallo family settled in Modesto around 1910 and Gallo wines continue to be headquartered here and our largest job provider. Agriculture remains strong, though today the main crops are almonds and walnuts. We've had our share of famous sons as well as the darker side of our earlier existence. In 1973, George Lucas made us famous with *American Graffiti.*

9th Street still has issues 150 years later. The "sins of our fathers" have a tendency to be systemic problems that we can all too often overlook or gloss over: "That's just the way it is." From economics to substance abuse, racial segregation, and more, the past lurks. I have found that sometimes we need to take a step back and look at our history. We need to understand it and name it so that we can do the hard work of overcoming it.

Catalyst for Change

The recession became, in a very real sense, the catalyst for all of the good that would happen later. It was, like Sebastian Junger said, the crisis that forced all of us—city and county officials, churches, nonprofits, businesses, individuals—to change, to look beyond ourselves and do something. The seeds were there, the recession was what allowed those seeds to germinate. It didn't happen overnight and all of us had a lot to learn, a lot to unlearn.[5]

I had a lot to unlearn myself, and that hit home for me in a very unexpected way. A foster agency in town wanted to have a Christmas party for their kids and resource families. They were trying to find some place to have the party and they really didn't have any money to do it. I got connected with them through my wife and let them know, "hey, I'm on staff at this big church and I can sign off on it and give you a free room." So there I am, walking around the church campus, showing this foster agency director the different room options where her group can have this party. We kept going to different buildings. She had never been to anything like this huge church and school before. She sees all these sprawling buildings, all these options for rooms. And she is floored by it all. I will never forget what she said, because it haunts me to this day.

---

5   As I think about everything that has gone on from about March of 2020 until now, I can't help but see the parallels. Crisis can become a catalyst for good. This time it's a pandemic and racial tensions not to mention politics, but the same thing can happen.

"This is f---ing Disneyland! Where are you?" I'm paraphrasing now, but just a little. "You're on this big, beautiful campus. There's people around you that need help, kids that need homes. I need families to step up and help. Clearly you have the means. I thought that the church was about taking care of people in need."

And she wasn't wrong.

There were probably a hundred moments during that time period where I kept asking myself "what are we doing? The city's on fire and where are we?" But that moment, that conversation is the one that remains forever etched in my mind and my heart. The danger was clear to me: as things continue to get worse "out there", it's easy to hunker down in our church to be safe. We have our cafeteria, we can get coffee, we can send our kids to school here. We can just never leave this little Disneyland world because things are getting so bad out there. But I knew that's not the kind of life that I wanted to live. That's not the way of Jesus as I understood it. And I knew that our church really didn't believe that either. After all, I had been hired to bring those community engagement events we had been doing in the college group to the whole church. I knew a lot of people in the church that were kind, compassionate people, people who actually did care. But we clearly had a problem.

Shortly after I got hired as outreach pastor, I got the book *Externally Focused Church* by Eric Swanson and Rick Rusaw. In it, they ask a simple question. I'm not sure if it's original with them, but it's where I first heard it. Basically, the question is this: *"If the church were to disappear, would anyone miss it? Would anyone notice or care?"*

The question wouldn't leave me alone. I was afraid I knew the answer. I grew up in church. I went to a Christian college and grad school. I became a college pastor. Now I was an outreach pastor. I was surrounded by church people. Looking back, I have to admit something: growing up I don't remember anyone I knew volunteering at local organizations or spontaneously helping a family in need much less talking about the need to do so. And the more I thought about the question the more troubled I became.

The book had such an impact on me that I had my assistant order a bunch of copies for me. The thing was, at the same time I moved roles from college pastor to outreach pastor, she moved from being my assistant to the assistant for the senior pastor. She was still working with me a little bit in the transition, but in the confusion of the transition, she thought the request was from the senior pastor. She ordered the book for all the elders of the church and for the main church staff and when they came in, rather than giving them to me, she handed them out to everyone. They all read it, thinking it was from the senior pastor when it was actually from me. Bob Ross would have called it a happy accident; I think God moves in mysterious ways.

Things were stacking up in a pretty clear direction. The church leadership were already asking questions and had seen the need for something to change. The book added fuel to the fire and more and more of us were going "Whoa, what, who are we, who or what are we known for? We got to be more of a church outside of our walls, not just inside our walls."

I took a video camera around Modesto and asked over seventy people "What comes to mind when you think of Big Valley Grace Community Church?" The answers were staggering. Over 50 people had never heard of it. A little over 15 had either heard the name but not much else or were very negative, even sharing how they had been hurt by the church. Two, (*TWO!*), had both heard of the church and had good things to say about it—we had helped their family out.

That video became a part of a sermon that I delivered to our church. It was another step down the path toward community engagement. It forced us to ask the question, "What are we going to do about this?"

The recession made it clear to us that the community needed us to act, to be involved. It needed us, as the church, to actually love our city. It kept showing up in different ways. There were infrastructure issues and desperation. The city and county governments had to cut staff because of the crisis which only made matters worse. Our city was bleeding, hemorrhaging really. The community needed us to step up.

But even though our church leadership recognized the problem and the need, even though people in the church were starting to recognize that we had a responsibility to our city, there was a disconnect. Somehow the things we had done as a college group were not translating well. During that first couple of months as outreach pastor, we started a program called First Saturdays. The idea was simple: on the first Saturday of the month, as a church we would go out into the community to interact with the homeless. Not just hand out food, but actually be with them. The food, the water, whatever, it was a vehicle to talk to them and treat them with dignity. It was so good. We met some of the most amazing people, some incredible stories of people. The guy from Stanford whose wife left him. He was on our streets. He was a professor at Stanford who just gave up. There were all these cool stories and heartbreaking stories of the people we met, but it wasn't capturing the heart of the church.

Over a period of about a year we did it 8 times. It was working on me big time. The problem was there were only about 10 people of the thousands from the church who showed up on any given week, and that 10 included my wife and kids! It was clear that our approach needed to change. But it was more than just the approach.

As far as our Modesto city leaders were concerned, the church had simply gone away. That was what that foster care director thought for sure. The truth of the matter is, that was never entirely true, but it was a lot truer than many of us would like to admit. Don't get me wrong, I am not saying that the church, my church, wasn't doing great things. It was. I was part of a lot of them. But there was a disconnect. A disconnect between "us" and "them". A disconnect between the church and the community.

It began to dawn on me that I was fighting the wrong battle. I could see the problem; a lot of people could see the problem. It wasn't that people were cold hearted. Sure, there were some who thought "I pay my taxes, isn't it the government's job to take care of that?" I think that a lot of people were simply overwhelmed. They had no idea of what to do. A program like First Saturdays was just that, a program. And it was intimidating for a lot of people who aren't like me. I am a pioneer; I like to go blazing into uncharted territory and start new things. Lots of people, probably most people aren't like that. Anybody who knows me will tell you that I am an over-the-top extrovert. I can and do talk to just about anybody. I love it. Again, lots of people aren't like that. For many, the idea of committing to spend a Saturday morning every month to this program was more than they were willing to bite off. And I had to admit, "First Saturdays" wasn't exactly a compelling idea. It told people when we met, not why or even what we were doing. So we took a step back, started pulling threads together and realized that we needed a rallying cry. We needed more than just a program. We needed to remember that, after all, our community was us. We needed something tangible to start to reclaim our voice.

Love Modesto

We went back to the drawing board. What were we actually trying to accomplish? How could we do that better? We wanted people to get involved in the community—outside the walls of the church. So we decided to scale back the number of events and at the same time broaden our appeal and impact. Something that would connect at a heart level. We landed on a church-wide volunteer day that would make a tangible difference.

Through all of this, those doggone "Modesto Sucks!" t-shirts were still stuck in my mind. And then I stumbled upon something that was far more insightful than I realized. As a total joke, I thought, "what if we came up with 'I Love Modesto' shirts." I gotta be honest, I was partly mocking those kids and their t-shirts, but I was also looking for a marketing hook.

The idea wasn't exactly original. Everyone has seen the "I love New York" shirts. I was looking for something like that, something that people would see, would want, and more importantly would become a way to build momentum and rally around.

At that time, I was tracking with Imago Dei Church in Portland. They had done something they called Love Portland. All of this is flashing through my head: the joke, the New York shirts and then Love Portland.

I remember thinking, "Love Portland. Love Modesto. That's it. That's the name, Love Modesto."

We started promoting this volunteer day at our church months ahead of time. We did all kinds of wacky things. We handed out T-shirts, we came up with "I Love Modesto" decals, we did photo booths with an "I Love Modesto" banner. It wasn't a big thing. It doesn't seem terribly important when I look back. But it was real. It was a start. And it tapped into something that I should have seen all along.

People love their cities.

Or at least a significant enough portion of them do. Peter Kageyama, researcher and author of *For the Love of Cities*, argues that typically 10% of people are "angry, disengaged and hostile towards their city", at the other end of the bell curve are about 10% who "love their city and [are] actively supporting, promoting and creating for it." But it is the middle portion that really matters. They may be bored, curious or somewhat neutral, but underneath, if they can be motivated, they really do love their cities.[6]

Since those first years we have found out that it really doesn't matter who you are or where you are from, chances are you love your city. Most people love where they are from. It gives them a sense of identity, of belonging. Those worst cities lists? We were put on there by outsiders. People who didn't know us. Who weren't us. And the people at Big Valley Grace were about to blow my mind with just how much they cared.

The first Love Modesto event happened in March of 2009. We had a total of 8 projects lined up: working with Habitat for Humanity, cleaning up local parks, doing yard work for people who needed it, getting donations for the food bank, helping local students, handing out hot chocolate to the homeless, (and to anyone walking or jogging through the park really), bringing carnations to hospitals and retirement homes, and a prayer team. I was hoping for 100 people. Looking back that seems ridiculously low given the size of our church and the amount of time and

---

6   Peter Kageyaema, from a personal email, December 12, 2020. See also www.fortheloveofcities.com.

energy we spent promoting the event, but you have to remember, that was 10 times the number of people who were coming out for First Saturdays.

1200 people showed up.

It was amazing. The people came through. They hadn't needed a program; they had needed something tangible to grab on to. I wasn't the only one seeing the problem. Not by a long shot. Do the math: 1200 people, 8 projects, that's 150 people per project. Honestly it was too many people per project—we didn't have the capacity for that many bodies at any one project. We were so overwhelmed we ended up telling the overflow people "go around town and see where there is something you can do and do it."

What we found that very first year and in the next several years was that people were hungry for a way to contribute. From the very beginning we received what I like to call "favor" from all kinds of directions. You will hear the stories in the coming pages, but every time I think about it, I am floored. Churches, other faith groups, those with no faith, city and county government, businesses, service clubs, school districts, young, old, rich, poor—they have all contributed, all been a part of helping us become what we are today. They have all loved our city.

To this day, I have a file that contains responses to that first event. Most of them are from people who volunteered. They were blown away by what serving others did not just for the people being served, but for them. A group of guys spent the entire day repairing the front steps of an elderly lady and the entire neighborhood was watching them throughout the day. Another guy shared his joy at teaching kids tennis. I have all kinds of stories, stories of people who were afraid to go out and interact with people, stories about young and old working side by side, but perhaps the one that hits me the most was a simple statement from a volunteer whose entire family was moved to change because they participated: "If BVG never did this again, we are making this part of who we are. God was at work in letting the individuals we encountered know that they are not invisible and matter to Him; that He cares for them."

That was what we wanted. That was at the heart of all of this. It makes me tear up just a little thinking about it all these years later.

We ended up doing three events in 2009 and two in 2010. People were excited. Remember, this was an event put on by one church, but as early as the second event, word started to get out. I personally went to a city council meeting to apologize for not always having the ownership or pride to get involved in my community, to share what we had done and to invite them to join us at the next event in July. We had a few people from other churches and from the city at the second event in the summer of 2009.

Part of the reason we scaled back in 2010 was that the fall event didn't get as much traction. We still had a bunch of people, (including new people), but overall, it just wasn't as well attended or as effective. Plus, from an organizational standpoint it was simply too much for the small staff that we had working on it. This was only one part of my job, and it was clearly taking over more than anyone expected.

It took us three years to figure out that even two events were too many. In our zeal to do stuff for the community we were actually blunting our effectiveness. Each time we did an event in the spring we got more people to show up, but the second event was not as well attended. What we soon realized was there was something magic about having one big, annual event. I think there are three main reasons for this.

First, the more events you have, the more the people who volunteer (and the people leading) can get fatigued. Signs go up, emails go out, you try to gear people up and the response is kind of like "didn't we just do this?" And the answer, honestly, is "well, yeah, we did, didn't we?"

Second, having a single annual event lowers the barrier to entry for most people. There are a few people who will just jump right in and sign up to volunteer once a week at the mission or helping the homeless, but that's not true for most of us. Most of us are willing to sign up for a one-time event, to get exposed to the mission, or helping the homeless or working with kids, or whatever it is. And if we go once and get a taste of it, get the tour and it isn't too overwhelming or threatening, well, then we are far more likely to go again.

But I think the third thing is actually the biggest factor. When we moved to a one time a year volunteer day, things exploded for us. There are several reasons for that, but the biggest is that we made it an event. Think about it this way, major holidays only happen once a year, the Super Bowl only happens once a year. When an opportunity to serve becomes an event like that, it brings the magic. People aren't just going out to volunteer; they are going to be a part of something bigger than themselves. And when it's for the city you love? That's a game changer.

Here's what it looked it looked like in practical terms:

2009: 3 events with 2800 total volunteers
2010: 2 events with 2500 total volunteers
2011: 2 events with 2850 total volunteers

That's not too shabby for one church, even a big one to pull off. We were doing lots of good things, we were helping lots of people. But in 2012, everything changed. We moved to a single event and had over 3500 volunteers. Since 2012 we have had more volunteers every single year. Moving to a single event was a really big part of that, but it wasn't the only thing. As early as year two we realized something: it wasn't just us.

It's Not Just Us

"In this life we cannot do great things. We can only do small things with great love."

— Mother Teresa

The older I get, the more I realize that people are not really all that different from one another. We may have different backgrounds, different ethnicities or political affiliations, even different religions and we can still have tons of things in common. Frankly, it's one of the big reasons why Love Our Cities works. People love where they are from. They can be really loyal, even relentlessly loyal to where they came from. Most of us know someone, maybe a neighbor or coworker, who is from somewhere else. They may have lived in their "new" city for half of their life or more, but they still root for their "hometown" team; they still think of themselves as a New Yorker even though they moved away when they were 12. Maybe they rebel against the way things are done in the new place or whatever. It's remarkable really, but we have all seen it, we all know that person. Why? Because people love where they are from. And it's not just something based in nostalgia.

We learned just how much people love their cities almost from the beginning of Love Modesto. Very early in the game, we learned that people were aching to be involved in *their* communities. By year two of Love Modesto, word was starting to get out about what we were doing. By the time we did our spring event in year three (2011), three additional cities had launched their own events with our help and using our model. The next year it jumped to 23. And all of it based out of our small office at one church. That kind of growth in that short of a span doesn't simply come from a brilliant idea or working hard or one church. There was a whole lot more going on at the same time. Simplifying in the extreme, it came down to three "C's": *Other Cities, Other Churches,* and *Other Constituencies.*

Other Cities

When we started Love Modesto, it was a church-wide volunteer day for our city, the one where we were physically located. I had no idea, not even a clue, that it would become a much broader thing. You have to realize, this was one part of my job and I was looking for something, anything really, that would actually work. We were doing it on a shoestring and making it up as we went. As we were headed toward the second year, someone came up with the idea of giving out yard signs for people. They were really simple, and we still use the same basic idea today: the Love Modesto logo and a date for the event. Simple, and as we have found, effective.

I remember standing at the door of the church after the service, promoting Love Modesto. I'm handing these yard signs out to anyone who will take them. I was talking to a lady from the church, involved, committed, but she wouldn't take a sign. She was from Ceres, the town just south of Modesto across the Tuolumne River. I will never forget what she said to me: "I don't want to put a Modesto sign in my yard. You come up with a Love Ceres and *then* I'll put a sign in my yard."

Until that moment it had never even occurred to me to think about other cities. It was just Modesto. Given the size of our church, how many different cities we had people coming from, I should have recognized it, but I didn't. I had never really thought much about how the pride that people showed in Modesto was there in all these other cities as well. I was so focused on the needs I saw in my city, so interested in creating solutions that I missed the very thing that was working on my own heart—the pretty universal desire of people to get involved, to help, in the places they are from. People love where they are from. Now I recognize it, but I didn't then. Thankfully, I didn't let my singular focus get in the way of what really was the start of Love Our Cities.

In a moment of God-directed clarity, I looked at her and asked, "Do you want to lead it?" Her response was, "well, let me talk to my husband. He's the fire chief in Ceres." It didn't take long for them to get back to me and say, "We're in, we'll lead Love Ceres." It felt natural. We used the same basic branding we had developed for Love Modesto, and I began helping them to start the process of developing Love Ceres.

About the same time one of the camera guys who helped film some of what was going on with Love Modesto, a member at Big Valley came to me. "Jeff, I live in Riverbank. My wife and I were talking, what would it take to do a Love Riverbank? We're really involved in Riverbank and we would like to see something like this there."

So here I am, still pretty new to the position, just over a year into this Love Modesto thing, and I have requests from people in the cities just north and just south of Modesto to help them do something similar. It dawned on me pretty quickly that we had stumbled on to something even bigger than I thought. Our big event for the spring of year two hadn't even happened yet and I am getting these requests! It blew me away.

It's funny how things that you never would have expected to impact you, dots you never would have connected, impact the way you look at things later. I grew up around the world of franchising. My parents owned a Dairy Queen, so that model of doing things was sort of baked into my thought patterns. Honestly it saved my bacon.

The idea of working in the community, even of mobilizing churches to engage with their communities is not exactly new or unique. Not far away from us was a church that was doing very similar things, they were successful at engaging people to actually get out into their city to work for change. People from other cities started to approach them and they, being the generous people that they were, said sure. But they tried to run it all themselves from one centralized hub and they couldn't keep up.

Because our approach was different, essentially a franchise model in many ways, we have been able to sustain what we do. The key for us has been a simple mentality—it's not about us. We purposefully decentralized leadership and empowered local leaders from the very beginning. This wasn't any grand or revolutionary discovery on my part. The reason why franchising works in the business world is simple: local owners have skin in the game. When I was approached by people from Ceres and Riverbank my response was simple: "Hey, it's your city. You care about it. It's your home. We will help you, but you are going to do it."

These two cities, just north and just south of Modesto, were in many ways natural extensions of what we were doing because the people starting them were a part of our church. They were next door with natural connections. We were a church that pulled people from a lot of different areas. People who are connected to each other in an organic way like a faith community are going to have things in common. But Ceres and Riverbank weren't the only two cities that approached me in year two.

Other Churches

Ceres and Riverbank were other cities, but it was still "our" church. Love Modesto was a Big Valley initiative. *We* were going out into the community. We were putting signs in our yards. People from our church were doing the work and leading the projects. We had the rally at our church. Just like it hadn't dawned on me to think about other cities, it also hadn't dawned on me to think about getting other churches on board with the idea and to be a part of it. On one level that just makes sense, I worked on staff at a specific church in a specific city. We also weren't looking to get people to come to our church—especially people from other churches—we wanted to get people from our church into the community to help. Of course, on another level it totally did make sense to get other churches involved because I knew that there were a lot more people in those churches who felt the same way we did.

For over ten years as a pastor in town I had developed relationships with all sorts of people from all sorts of different walks of life–especially other pastors. We met together for prayer meetings and retreats, sometimes we worked on different projects together. These people challenged and mentored me, they helped me become better at what I was doing, we read the same books and asked a lot of the same questions, all that sort of thing. Somewhere along the way I had mentioned what we were doing at some of those meetings. I had no intention at all to recruit anyone to be a part of what we were doing, but I am pretty sure that, me being me, I invited them to come see what we were up to. You know "Hey, you can come too, anybody's welcome." Word was getting out.

And so, in the second year, we started to get people from other churches showing up. A pastor in Escalon, a city a bit farther north of Modesto, came to the rally that second spring. I remember after everyone was released, he hung around and said, "hey, I'm Jim Davis. I pastor a church in Escalon. Could you help us get this thing going in Escalon? What would that look like?"

He wasn't alone. A lot of people from other churches had shown up that second year. In fact, the sanctuary at Big Valley could seat 1500 people, and we maxed it out. People love their city. People wanted to do something good for their city even if they weren't a part of our church. They wanted to know how this thing worked so they could replicate it in their own cities. As I reflected on that day, I realized that we were going to have to move the event out of Big Valley. We didn't have the space, and increasingly it was becoming apparent that because we were pulling in people from other churches, we were going to need a more neutral space, somewhere that everyone could feel connected to.

Because we were a big church in town, we had the resources to do things that other, smaller churches just didn't. I want to be very clear, that's not a slam on Big Valley or on big churches in general, nor is it intended to be a slight on smaller churches. Neither could be farther from the truth. Big Valley has a long history of being generous and helping other churches in the Modesto area. Their heart for others was, and remains, great. The thing was, because of who we were, both as the big church in town and because we were independent, it was really easy to overlook the involvement of others and to create tensions that we had no idea we were creating.

As more people from other churches started coming, we had pastors quietly asking, "Hey, do we have to do this here? We are already losing people to your church and if we have to have it here, I don't want to lose more." We certainly didn't intend to cause that kind of issue, but it was there.

So, in our third year, both for logistical reasons and because we saw that we had a genuine opportunity to involve other churches and really the whole community to a greater degree, we decided to move the rally. We realized that we had to be in a neutral place because Love Modesto wasn't about us, it was about *loving* Modesto. It was about the community and that meant not just our church but all the churches who wanted to be a part of it.

That may seem obvious, but you have to remember that there are reasons that there are all these different churches. Different denominations have different doctrinal beliefs, there are different approaches to worship styles and a host of other things that an outsider might never see but mean a lot to the people on the inside. All of that to say, cooperation among churches is something that most of us agree to in principle but have a harder time working out in practice. There can be a bit of a gang mentality, an "us versus them" thought process that creeps in. By moving away from Big Valley and to a neutral location we essentially stopped any potential turf wars.

When we made this move, not only did we make it easier for other churches to get involved, but we also multiplied our effectiveness. We increased the number of volunteers we got as well as the number (over 6 times as many) and kinds of projects we were able to do. We increased the connections in the wider community too.

At the same time, it wasn't just other churches that were showing up.

Other Constituencies

As I mentioned in the last chapter, the summer of our first year as I led an invocation at our city council meeting, I also offered an apology to the Modesto city leaders for not being more involved. I invited them to come to see what we were doing. A few came.

One of my favorite memories of our second year is also the least likely of any of them. I was doing an interview on a local radio station about the event. I was talking to the producer off air, and he told me "you know, I love what you're doing, and I love a lot of these projects." Then he said, "I'm glad. I feel like you've included people like me."

"What do you mean by that?"

"Well, straight up, I'm an atheist. I don't believe at all like you believe. And I think a lot of churches do a lot of good things, but honestly, I never feel welcomed. I don't feel like I can contribute, like I can be a part. But this thing right here, I feel like I can be a part of this. I even signed up for a project."

"Really? What project did you sign up for?"

"Singing hymns to seniors."

That was the project he signed up for. I was floored.

And I was like, "Wow." Like, "Why did you sign up for that project?"

"Well, because I grew up in, had some church background and I grew up, you know, just singing and around old people. It just felt like the right thing to do."

I still get goosebumps. This is exactly what I lived for. There's a lot of talk in church circles about the decline of the church, of people seeing it as irrelevant to their lives, but here was something that connected on a deep, deep level to someone who was never going to walk into a church otherwise.

He wasn't alone. Once word began to spread, even in year two, we were getting people who really weren't connected to the church at all, but they wanted to help. They loved their city too. We were still doing everything out of the church. This giant matrix of things was swirling around us: people from other cities wanted to do this, other churches were getting involved, and even an atheist radio producer wanted to help out by singing hymns to people at the retirement center! I may be slow, but I'm not dumb. Wow! This thing is bigger than I thought or dreamed, way broader too. This simple volunteer day was starting to reach people and catch on. It is infectious. People saw that they could actually make a difference in their city and they got excited. They wanted to be a part of it. Honestly, I think it changed them as much as they were able to change the city. So we started to look for a new venue.

Modesto is a decent sized city, but not extremely large, we are about 215,000 or so people. We had high school stadiums and the football field at the junior college, we even looked at using the local minor league baseball stadium for a place to meet. For one reason or another, none of them really worked for what we wanted to do. We needed a place that was central, accessible, and had a lot of parking. Somewhere along the line someone tossed out the idea of meeting in front of the Gallo Center, which is a big performing arts center right downtown. I am pretty sure I didn't come up with the idea, and it ended up being a perfect venue for us. Year 3, the first year we moved out of the church, we shut down four city blocks and had a big rally right there.

The move to the center of town gave us more than a bigger place to fit everyone and the opportunity to include other churches, it really grew awareness for the wider community. We started thinking bigger, we started getting the word out in new and innovative ways. We got permission to put up 4' X 8' signs all around town with the same branding we had used in the previous two years on our yard signs. They were impossible to miss, and they got everyone talking, and I mean everyone. Pretty soon the TV affiliates were calling and asking what was going on and things kept snowballing. Clearly the move was good for everyone because we jumped from just over 1200 people to well over 1700 people that spring.

Honestly, as I look back on it right now, I almost have to laugh. There was so much coming at me all at once, so much coming at the small group of people who were supporting this thing. Everything was blowing up at once. More churches involved, more people from the community, more cities, it was a wild ride. And I had no idea how much wilder it was going to get. We did two events in 2011, one in April and one at the end of June and we did them in all four cities simultaneously. It was awesome, then the floodgates opened.

A Bigger Challenge

It didn't take long for my phone to start ringing. I wasn't calling any-one; people were finding me. If anyone doubts the power of television to get the word out, I can tell you, it really does make a difference. I started getting calls from all over the central valley. I got calls from big cities and little ones, all of them within about 50 miles or so of Modesto. It also didn't take me too long to figure out that something was going to have to give. There was just no way that I could keep going in this direction without something changing.

I saw where things were headed so I had to have a conversation with the Executive Pastor of the church, Bobby Fisher.

"Bobby, hey we've got a decision to make here. The thing is, we're going to have a whole lot of cities getting on board here. I'm getting calls from all over. There are a lot of people who want to do this. If we keep going like this, I'm going to be spending a whole lot more time doing this and you gotta let me know right now if that's what you want. We can shut it down and just focus on Modesto or focus on just a few cities around us. Or do you want this thing to really go? Do you want me to keep going, to keep working with all these cities that contact us?"

"Hey, if God's doing this, man. Keep going for this."

"Okay, so you know what that means? Like I can't do as much of the other stuff. We had four cities this year and I'm starting to get more calls from more and more cities. Potentially, we could have a whole lot more next year. I'm going to be supporting these cities, giving website support, all kinds of stuff."

He was totally on board. Let me tell you, that's the kind of response you want from your boss when there is something that you are really passionate about. It was a risk for him too. We were using Big Valley's resources, spending money given to Big Valley. It made sense for us to expand to the cities right around us because we were a church that drew from all these places. Expanding further, that was something different because I was getting calls from places that had no connection to Big Valley.

Bobby had the vision to see that something bigger was going on and he recognized we had a chance to get on board. It really was in the DNA of Big Valley. It's right in the name of the church actually. "Big Valley" meant the whole of it—the original plan was to plant a bunch of churches up and down the valley. That plan changed over time, but in a way, it came true: I had people tell me "Hey we are having an impact up and down the big valley." It was a really cool thing to see that heartbeat lived out and I am so grateful that this one church saw the possibilities, was willing to dream big and let me devote myself to this thing.

We had no idea just how important that conversation and decision was. By the time our fourth year was in full swing, there were 23 cities on board and doing their own events. Five times growth in a single year. Over the next couple of years we saw even more expansion, we started partnering with cities around the country, we found more projects and made more connections both in Modesto and elsewhere. We learned a lot, made a lot of mistakes, and kept moving forward.

The whole time we were growing as Love Modesto, there was even more going on inside of me. I was seeing a lot of things I hadn't seen before. I was asking lots of questions of myself and others. They were asking questions too. I was going through the wringer professionally, personally, and spiritually. The biggest question was both simple and daunting, "What's Next?"

City Spotlight:
San Luis Obispo, California[7]

Year Joined: 2016
City Leaders: Stephanie Buresh and Chris Blake

Tell us a bit about your city:
San Luis Obispo, often referred to as SLO by locals, sits on the Central Coast of California approximately halfway between Los Angeles and San Francisco. The city was founded in 1776 by Spanish Franciscan priest Junipero Serra and is one of California's oldest European founded communities. Its namesake comes from the Mission that was named after the 13th-century saint and bishop, Louis of Toulouse. Today, San Luis Obispo is a city of approximately 48,000 residents and is the county seat for San Louis Obispo County which has a population of about 285,000 people.

What do you love about San Luis Obispo, and what are some of the unique challenges you face?
At one point, National Geographic and Oprah Winfrey declared San Luis Obispo the happiest place on earth. It is a community focused on outdoor recreation and health, education (California Polytechnic State University being one of the largest employers) and helping others. San Luis Obispo has the largest number of nonprofits per capita in the state of California. The city is always buzzing with justice focused events and celebrating the diversity of opinions and views. Although there is a vibrancy and beauty in our community, San Luis Obispo faces many challenges. Our city continues to be faced with a cost of living that surpasses what the average family can afford. We are one of the most expensive cities

---

7   The homepage of www.loveourcities.org has links to all of our partner city sites.

in California and the nation. Those issues have contributed to a rising number of homeless and hungry in our community.

How did you hear about Love Our Cities and how has Love Our Cities helped you?

Love SLO began with discussion on how to get high school students more aware of the community service opportunities in San Luis Obispo. At the time, we worked at Mission College Preparatory Catholic High School. One day when we were discussing ways to enhance service for our students, Chris was reminded of Love Modesto and the impact it had in his home community. We quickly decided to schedule a conference call with Love Our Cities founder Jeff Pishney. That call made us realize that we not only wanted to create Love SLO for our students but for the entire town of San Luis Obispo. This began our wonderful relationship with Love Our Cities and began our Love SLO ministry.

Tell us about your city-wide volunteer day:

Our city-wide volunteer day consists of approximately 50 different projects. We start our morning at a rally in the center of the city in the Mission plaza right at the steps of the building that founded our town. Our rally starts with a free pancake breakfast provided by the local fire fighters association. We have the local fire department with their trucks, police officers with their cars and ambulances present, for kids to explore and to show their support of the event. There is face painting and always a new and creative public art project for volunteers to express their appreciation for SLO. Once volunteers pick up their free t-shirt at our t-shirt booth, they can head over to our Love SLO backdrop to get a photo with their friends and family. Volunteers can be seen sipping the complimentary coffee, eating donuts, and joining in fellowship, while listening to upbeat music over the sound system. In between songs, we give morning updates and information about the day. Once we start getting close to service tip-off time, we gather everyone around a stage where we thank everyone for coming, talk about the great work volunteers are doing in our community, and encourage everyone to have a great day. Also, we have the Mayor share comments on the importance of a service day and then throw out four $50 envelopes, asking whoever gets the money to pay it forward to someone in need. Our final remarks help direct everyone to where they are going and then it's a mad dash to Love our City!

What others are saying:

"Overall a fantastic experience and an impressive, valuable event. What you have done is incredible, and it fills my heart with joy that something like Love SLO exists to make our beautiful city even better!"

"Being a part of this day was the best experience. Meeting new people from my city, getting to be with ones we know, and coming together for a great cause. Our community is amazing! Thank you for bringing this community together."

"The number of volunteers we had come out for the project was an overwhelming blessing. We were able to accomplish weeks' worth of work in just a few hours thanks to all those hands. Not to mention, we had a lot of people interested in returning to help in the future, the opportunity to share who we are as an organization and what we do in the community was incredible."

"It was amazing to meet and work alongside my fellow community members of all different ages and backgrounds. Also, to see the smiles, joy, and sense of accomplishment on each of our faces as we finished our project made me proud to be a part of Love SLO."

What's Next?

"Love is bigger than anything in its way."

— **U2**

When I think back to all that went on in those early years, all that led up to where we are now, it still seems a bit surreal. It's wild to remind myself of where we started and all that has happened since. In many ways, that conversation with Bobby Fisher about expanding what we were doing by including other cities set the stage for what came next. I didn't know it then, but in many ways that conversation became the catalyst for Love Our Cities.

Every once in a while, I go back through some of the video from the early days of Love Modesto. One of the things that struck me recently was the fact that early on I knew that one day wasn't enough. I even made comments to the news crews about knowing that we couldn't solve all the problems of our city in one day.

"What's next?" can be a perfectly legitimate question, one that propels you forward to get better, or, if you're not careful, it can turn dark. It can be the polite way of saying "what's one day going to do?". I have lost count of the times I have been asked that question. I would be lying if I said I never asked it myself. The city-wide volunteer event, that has become the hallmark of Love Our Cities, does great things for communities all around the country. I have seen it firsthand; I have witnessed it in the lives of people I have met over the past ten years, I have heard it in the stories of the cities who have partnered with us. I know that we do good things, that we help to make our communities better.

Even with all our early success, it didn't take long for people to start asking, "what good is one day?" For some it's an excuse—they really don't want to get involved. The question is really a way to offer an excuse that feels like an honest objection but in fact hides the truth. I have to confess that this kind of attitude irritates me, I really don't get it. I try to remember that those people have a story too. Often the people objecting the most loudly have been hurt themselves or taught to look at the world that way. I try to remember that, but it can be difficult.

If it were only people who didn't want to get involved, who were too self-absorbed to care, that raised the objection, well that would be pretty easy to ignore. The problem is that it's not just the people who don't care who were raising the question—it was *me*. I could see that there was some truth in the question.

One day could not solve the problems we were facing as a city. We could clean up a park and weeks or months later the trash would be back. We could offer a meal to a homeless person, but they would still be homeless. We *were* doing good things! I knew that we were helping. I knew that in small ways we were making our city better. Yes, there was always more to be done, and we could always do it better, but I could see it. I could see it in the faces of the people we helped. I could see it in the faces of the people who volunteered. I could see it in the fact that these other cities wanted to be a part of what we were doing, that we were growing by leaps and bounds.

Love Our Cities didn't have a name yet. It wasn't really a thing, but it was being born before my eyes. We were making a real difference and our influence was expanding, but I could see that my city still needed help.

Something was missing.

Holy Discontent

To be perfectly honest Love Modesto wrecked me. I simply couldn't go back to the way things were before. I couldn't just do church as usual, separate from the rest of my life, the rest of my week, from my relationships and the things that really mattered. Sunday faith wasn't good enough. Someone said, "when Jesus comes to town things should get better." I believe that. I believe it now and I believed it then. Love Modesto was the catalyst for changing me. There was a lot more to do. I wanted my faith to impact everything.

The thing about building something like Love Modesto is that you start seeing needs everywhere. When you start paying attention and trying to address the real needs of the real people in your community you start seeing those needs everywhere. What you are doing starts changing you as much as anyone you are helping.

There were lots of threads coming together in my life. I didn't know it then, but they were coming together in ways that would shape not only my life but what Love Modesto would become and how we could start addressing all of those needs that one day couldn't fix.

As a pastor, I had been thinking about outreach, reading books and going to conferences. It was impacting my faith. I was in touch with what was going on around the country, about issues that were pretty universal. They were the same things that I was seeing and hearing as we built Love Modesto. The more I got to know the organizations and the people around town that were actually trying to do things to help people, the more that I saw trends. The more of the volunteer days I led, the more I got to know the leaders in the community—from government services to the nonprofits that were working to help the community, to the schools and other churches—the more that I was coming to realize we needed to be doing something more. We needed to be thinking about things differently.

But it was more than a professional interest for me. It was personal. And it had started long before Love Modesto. My wife Karen is a social worker. In the middle of all of the stuff I did as a college pastor she was there. She wasn't just doing stuff with me. She was pushing me to become more than I was, to think about the implications of my faith and what we needed to do. It was the same in the new role and as Love Modesto grew. She pushed me. She was the reason that the foster care director ever came to my church looking for a place for a Christmas party—Karen worked there. She helped me to see what was in front of me. Our kids' school, our neighbors. She helped me to see that this had to be more than a campaign or a program. *We* had to get involved, to really love people in need. So we started the process of becoming foster parents and adopting.

These threads and more came together for me in one, very surprising, unexpected moment. I was hosting a Sunday service at the satellite campus for our church. We streamed video of the sermon from the main location. I had done my thing and was in the back when the sermon started. It was on the prayer of Jabez.

Even now I can't believe I am actually admitting to this. When the book *The Prayer of Jabez* came out and became an overnight bestseller I thought it was ridiculous. I didn't like the way so many people used it to spiritualize their own selfish desires. The fact that I was hearing this passage being preached on in my own church a decade later didn't exactly sit well with me. So there I am in the back, only halfway paying attention and having an almost allergic reaction to the message of "dream bigger, expand your blah, blah, blah" and something clicked.

All of the stuff that I had been experiencing over the last couple of years was just churning in my mind. As I sat there in the back of the auditorium, both annoyed by the sermon and somehow motivated by it, I began scribbling down notes. Lots and lots of notes. I was no longer paying much attention at all to what was being said. I was thinking and dreaming about what Love Modesto could actually do, could actually be. If we really want to have a long-lasting impact in the community it has to be more than just a day. I kept thinking about the things that we were doing with Love Modesto, the way that our brand had captured people's attention. Love was the operative word. The city-wide volunteer day was important—crucial even—but I was beginning to see that it was step one.

I looked at my notes and thought about it. I pulled out my phone and pulled up Go Daddy. Love Our Neighbors. Check. Bought it. Love Our Schools. Check bought it. Love Our Kids. Taken. Ugh. Love All Our Kids. Check bought it. Right then and there, I started seeing the future of Love Modesto, of where we were going. It was only a glimpse, but I was fully engaged.

The thing that was missing was sustainability.

Sustainability

We started Love Modesto because we wanted to help our community. We wanted people in our church to get out and actually do what Jesus asked—love their neighbor. The longer that Love Modesto operated, the more I realized that we were doing a lot of good, but we lacked sustainability. We needed an ongoing, systematic approach to systematic problems. I didn't realize it then, but part of the reason we had several church-wide and city-wide volunteer days in those early years is that we instinctively realized that just doing one day wasn't enough. We didn't really know the whys beyond it, but we gradually began to see that our instinct was right even though the execution was wrong.

We needed a way to turn the positive energy of the city-wide volunteer day into an ongoing movement. People felt good about helping. We needed to channel that energy into something more than just feeling good, more than just checking off the "I'm part of the solution" box. (For the record, I totally believe that people should feel good about helping. It's just not enough.)

About this same time, two different local school principals contacted me completely independently of one another. "Thanks for the help. Thanks for the projects your teams did. It was great and really appreciated. But if you really want to help our schools, well, we need more positive adult role models throughout the year. If you can figure out how to help get them to come in regularly and help our students, then you're truly going to be loving our schools."

Part of sustainability is connecting things that haven't been connected before. Connecting people that haven't been connected before. Love Modesto was becoming a connection point for people. I am a connector by nature. I love doing it and it just comes natural to me. When I first moved to Modesto I started connecting with people in my church and with people who led other churches. I got involved in City Ministry Network (www.cityministrynetwork.org) which led to great relationships with other pastors in town and with Marvin Jacobo who became a really important mentor for me. As Love Modesto grew, I naturally started meeting leaders of nonprofits in town as well as government and business leaders. Right smack in the middle of this I met Eric.

It was 2012, we were in the middle of year four when things were really beginning to take off. Eric and his family had begun attending our church. He had a background in business and had gone to seminary in San Diego. When he heard about what we were doing with Love Modesto, especially connecting to nonprofits he gave me a call. We started talking almost daily, bouncing ideas around, figuring things out. I didn't know it at the time, but those conversations would lead to much more.

Teachable

A big part of creating something sustainable is being teachable. We wanted to learn everything we could about the real problems that our community was facing. We wanted to make sure that we were engaging the right people in the right places in the right ways. Over the years we have tried to build a humble attitude and open spirit into everything that we do. Every year, we spend time reviewing the projects for our city-wide volunteer day. We make it a point to learn from what we have done. We review the categories and the specific projects; we check to see how volunteers are sticking (or not). We have learned a lot. We have learned just how vital our project leaders are, how the best ones follow up with the people who volunteered. We have seen firsthand how a good project leader ends up recruiting people for more than just a day. Lots of our volunteers come back to the same project year in and year out and a pretty significant percentage make that organization or project an ongoing part of their life.

Shortly after that Sunday service and my scribbled notes and domain name purchases, we put in motion a plan to launch ongoing initiatives around neighborhoods, kids and schools. These were some of the biggest issues and challenges our city was facing. In some ways the needs of neighborhoods, kids and schools are pretty universal, however, what those needs look like in any given city are going to change, sometimes dramatically. But again, I can't stress enough that the reason those three areas came to the forefront was because of the connections that I had made in the community, because I was listening to what was going on and learning. Even so we certainly made some missteps along the way.

Like I said before, I am a doer. My default is to see a problem and charge in to fix it. That doesn't always work out so well. We have made lots of mistakes along the way. Thankfully I have had some really good people around me. They have helped guide me and our team along the way and have helped us to become better at what we do.

When we started work on launching these other projects, we started with what we knew, what had worked for us—an event. Since neighborhoods are sort of mini cities, it was only natural for us to start there. We thought and brainstormed and dreamed and wondered what it would be like if we all got out in our front yards again. Be a front yard neighbor. Get out in your front yard, throw a party, get to know your neighbors, have a great time and all that. Yay! Great idea, right? So, we planned it and put the machine into motion.

Then Rosie Perez, who was in the Modesto police department got in touch with me and said, "Hey, do you know about something called a National Night Out? We do this in the first week of August every year."

"Yeah, I think I heard about that. You know, I don't know, I mean. . ." I was a bit sheepish.

"Yeah, well, it's kind of the same thing you're doing with this Love our Neighbors thing," Then she made it real, "you always want us to get on board with your stuff. Why don't you get on board with our stuff? This was happening way before what you are doing; you're duplicating our event."

And, I had to admit, "You're right Rosie, I'm wrong, we won't do this again. It'll end."

Now we do a Halloween event that doesn't compete. I've been working hand in hand with Rosie ever since that conversation. We have become friends. She promotes our Halloween event and we promote National Night Out for her. We made a mistake because we weren't paying attention, we were doing, but not listening. Because we were willing to admit it, we have an ally today and together we are doing much more than either of us could on our own. That is what sustainability is all about.

The growing pains have been real, but they have been important, they have helped us learn and become who we are. They have helped us define what it is that we do and why, what makes us unique and helped us to realize that what we are doing really can help people all over the place. We grew numerically in the early days, but I think we also grew up—got a lot more mature—too. In life growing up means that sooner or later you have to move out of mom and dad's house. As Love Modesto grew, we were forced to address an unanticipated issue. We were going to have to move out too.

Going Full Time

In a manner of months after Bobby Fisher and I had the conversation about seeing what God was up to, we were at 23 cities. Within another 12 months or so another conversation pushed us to the next phase. Bobby had moved on to other endeavors. There was a new executive pastor—also named Bobby, Bobby Kirchner. He had been observing everything that was going on. He saw the truth that I hadn't quite admitted to myself. This Love Modesto thing had mushroomed, it had taken over not just my time, but also my imagination and my heart.

"Jeff, you're checked out."

And he was right. I found my mind wandering in meetings. I found it hard to get to all the other things that I needed to do. Love Modesto and helping all these other cities had become more than a full-time job. As it grew it simply outgrew one church. I don't mean that in a bad way at all. It had simply spread so widely that it just wasn't feasible for one church to run it all. Big Valley Grace Community Church had a specific mission in a specific place. We were blowing past that by the nature of what we were becoming. And to their credit, they saw it and embraced it.

"Jeff, you need to start a non-profit. And we want to support you."

We've all heard horror stories about organizations, yes even churches, who get protective of territory, who want to maintain control and trample innovation. Big Valley had every reason to curtail what I was doing, what Love Modesto was becoming. But they didn't. They saw something big happening and wanted to put fuel on the fire, not douse it. They believed in what Love Modesto was becoming. I cannot stress this enough—they were incredible. They wanted to see this thing grow and they championed me and what we were doing. To this day Big Valley is a great supporter, Love Modesto was their baby. They birthed it. It simply would not be around today if they didn't get behind it and then launch me into this new thing.

In the fall of 2014, year four of our events and five years after the idea of the first Love Modesto event, we launched as our own non-profit. By this time Eric and I really were talking pretty much daily, and it really made perfect sense for him to be one of the founding board members. To be perfectly honest I was using up way more of his time than I had any right to do, but it worked out for the best in the end. I was on my own in a little office shepherding Love Modesto and a bunch of other cities.

By the time 2016 rolled around and we were two years into the non-profit, there were about 30 cities. We had a five-page manual, a website that was a little clunky but functional. The problem was that what was built originally for one or two cities was fine, but at 30 cities, it was really beginning to break. We didn't really have much bandwidth to resource and help our cities grow. That September Eric was on vacation down in

Monterey, but we were still having our daily conversation and I said I think the next hire would be someone that could partner with me to run the city expansion so I could focus on what was happening in Modesto. Eric was the obvious choice and transitioned from a board member to City Engagement Director October 1st.

What Eric brought to the table, beyond just the need for more bodies to get things done, was a platform to bring Love Our Cities to scale. By this point he really knew how I thought, he helped me to think better about the things that were going on and he brought things to a whole new level—from establishing a website platform each city could utilize independently, to building our online leadership training center and helping flesh out what sustainability looks like for our neighborhoods, schools, and kids' initiatives. All of this has really helped us to become who we are today. It has opened up the possibilities for us to truly help cities across the country. It has helped us to think through why we do what we do, how we do it, and what the things that we do look like.

That's our story. Let's get on to the next stage—laying a solid foundation so that you can love your city.

City Spotlight:
Colorado Springs, Colorado

Year joined: 2018
City Leaders: Stu Davis and Corrie Smith

Tell us a bit about your city:
Located near the base of Pikes Peak, Colorado Springs is located on Colorado's front range at an elevation of over 6000 feet. Colorado Springs lies 60 miles south of Denver and is the state's second largest city with a population of almost 480,000 and a metro area population of 740,000.

A variety of industries, including national defense, technology, and manufacturing, have created a stable and growing economy. Pikes Peak, known as "America's mountain," acts as a gateway to the mountains for outdoor recreation and ecotourism of all kinds. National attractions such as the United States Olympic Training Center and Olympic Hall of Fame draw hundreds of thousands of people here every year. Five military installations, including the United States Air Force Academy and NORAD mean that tens of thousands of soldiers, airmen, and their families from across the globe call Colorado Springs home.

Colorado Springs is often referred to as the "mecca" of Christian non-profits. In 1991, James Dobson relocated Focus on the Family's headquarters here and many others soon followed. Today, dozens of national and global ministries consider Colorado Springs their home base including Compassion International, Outreach Inc., Young Life, and the Navigators. To those on the outside, Colorado Springs appears to be a bastion of evangelical Christendom, but those of us who live here understand there is a more complex history and story unfolding in the shadow of Pikes Peak.

***What do you love about Colorado Springs, and what are some
of the unique challenges you face?***
Colorado Springs is a wonderful place to call home. Tens of thousands of active-duty and retired military personnel provide daily
reminders of the incredible costs at which our freedoms have come.
The robust community of faith provides fertile ground for many
services and support structures for people who are struggling. I
love this city. But while we enjoy many of the pillars that make a
community strong, Colorado Springs struggles to accurately see
and deal with a number of challenges facing our country.

Manitou Springs, a western borough of our city nestled underneath
the Pikes Peak highway, was once one of the nation's hotspots for
occult activity. The military culture can be incredibly challenging
for young families, often creating environments where domestic
violence, suicide, and substance abuse can creep in.

Overall, Colorado Springs is more than 80% white. Minority
community members often have a difficult time finding a foot-
hold in community conversations. The majority-white neighborhoods across our city are filled with good people who are discon-
nected from the larger conversations around race, inequity, and
marginalization. As a result, communities of color are often con-
fined to under-resourced school districts and job opportunities
that keep them out of the social mix and engender the downward
spiral of poverty.

At the same time, Colorado Springs is in a period of rapid, nearly
uncontrollable growth. The metro area has grown by 20% in the
last decade, and nearly 50% since 2000. We are struggling to figure out how to be a big city, and to find ways to be both smarter
and more compassionate to the broad spectrum of people moving
here from all over the country. This growth has contributed to

an uprising of vocal liberal groups reacting to ultra-conservative movements pulling at the fabric of our efforts to build community and health in our city. Those who consider Focus on the Family and its peer organizations models of Christian engagement are met with our city's most frequently seen bumper sticker: "Focus on your own damn family." As a result, Colorado Springs is, like many other cities, a deeply divided place. For the local church, it's a season filled with opportunity, but also with great challenges.

How did you hear about Love Our Cities and how has Love Our Cities helped you?

COSILoveYou first connected with Love Our Cities in 2018. Our volunteer management platform wasn't robust enough for our growing CityServe Day. We had thousands of people wanting to serve Colorado Springs and we couldn't find a volunteer platform that allowed us to steward the involvement of that many volunteers well. That's when we found Love Our Cities. They had built a volunteer platform for their own service day that boasted many of the elements that we were looking for, and they understood the work that we were doing. They understood the heart of city transformation.

While we initially connected about their volunteer management platform, we have been encouraged to be a part of the larger movement of leaders, churches, and nonprofits connected to Love Our Cities. We have been able to connect with additional City Gospel Movements (www.citygospelmovements.org) and learn from other leaders doing similar work. We share the same struggles and find ways to encourage and sharpen each other in a journey that is still finding its legs. The team at Love Our Cities has advocated for our movement and has always been a phone call away if we needed any additional support.

Tell us about your city-wide volunteer day and other efforts you have undertaken:

Our CityServe Day has allowed the local church in Colorado Springs to begin to change the way it is perceived in our city. Rather than being known for what we do on Sundays, the church is starting to find ways to connect with ways to meet tangible needs across our community throughout the year. Homelessness, poverty, hunger, and racial inequities are not unique to Colorado Springs, but thanks to the mass-movement of thousands of believers loving and serving their city, city leaders are beginning to recognize that the church has much to offer and can be a trusted partner for city transformation. We are the largest one-day volunteer effort in our city and are always asking city leaders what else can be done. When those leaders see armies of people marching out in love not protest, we become a force for good and are invited into other conversations.

What others are saying:

"When we can come together and lock arms, there's no greater expression of unity and loving one another."

—Brandon Cormier, Pastor, Zeal Church

"When you think about volunteering, you think it can be kinda scary, but I'm so glad that I just dove right in because I had the best time. I made new friends and serving is an all-around good feeling."

—Paula Wulf, CityServe Day Volunteer

"I have volunteered with this organization for the past three years. My experiences were great and it's a wonderful way to be involved in the local community. Will definitely continue to volunteer in as many opportunities as I can."

—Ann S., CityServe Day Volunteer

"As someone who works for the City of Colorado Springs, COSI-LoveYou has found many ways to positively impact our local government, partnering with many of our departments to clean storm water channels, clean up parks, and beautify our city with flowerbeds. COSILoveYou has helped to unite the different faith communities in Colorado Springs to do more together than they could ever do apart. They have been exceptional to work with, maintaining a level of professionalism that is refreshing. Few organizations have the level of thoughtfulness and care they have, and they have been a wonderful non-profit partner for the entire city—whether that is in city services, supporting our school systems, or simply bringing neighbors together through a common cause. I would highly recommend the people of COSILoveYou for any project work that might fit their scope"

–Joe H. , CityServe Day Volunteer,
Colorado Springs City Employee

"COSILoveYou is an incredible organization unifying so many different churches in our community under a common mission to love our city in practical ways. . .. I have found COSILoveYou to be an invaluable resource to connect pastors, churches, and communities. . .. We love partnering with COSILoveYou!"

– Joe Adams, Pastor, Manna Church

Part 2:

Why, How, and What

All of us, on some level, want to make a difference in the world. It's baked in. Both Eric and I, and really all the people we have worked with over the years, have felt it. We believe it. It's at least a part of why we keep doing this. Our story is important, the story of how we got here. So is yours. Something brought you to this book, on some level you connect with what we are talking about or you wouldn't have lasted this long.

Here's the thing, there are a lot of really good people in the world with really good ideas to help their communities, to "make things better". Lots of people *want* to help. All kinds of people. Sometimes their ideas get off the ground and fizzle out. Sometimes they never get off the ground at all.

"Why does Love Our Cities work?"

We get asked that question a lot. There are probably a lot of different ways to answer the question. It would not be honest of us to say that personality and drive have nothing to do with it, they do. I am a connector, a motivator. I am a pioneer by nature—I don't want to be a settler. I want to make things happen. Eric is an organizer, the guy who looks at the vision and says, how can we make this happen and happen better? He thinks things through and coaches people through the details. But neither of our personalities are enough to sustain something like what Love Our Cities has become.

As we planned this book, we talked through the ingredients of our success. There are several principles that come to the surface for us when we get asked about our ability to grow and sustain Love Modesto and then Love Our Cities. We have had cities partner with us and drop off. Some of them are coming back. Jim Collins is famous for telling organizations that they have to have the right people on the bus and then get them in the right seats. We totally agree, and sometimes the reason those cities are coming back is because the people running things had the right vision, but they were in the wrong seat. It happens. But there is another thing that can be a problem. To use a different metaphor, the foundation is flawed so the building ultimately collapses.

Both of us are pretty practical guys. It's tempting to just dive into the nuts and bolts—here's the 10-step plan to start a city-wide volunteer day in your city. We could do that. Lots of people do. The problem with that approach is that you end up with a bunch of practices but none of the underlying principle. In the end it would be doing you a disservice. It is precisely because we want this book to be practical that we have to start with these foundational principles. The really cool thing is that we have found these foundational principles have not only strengthened us as an organization, they have also helped us to grow as individuals. In the end they are incredibly practical.

You are probably familiar with Simon Sinek's "Golden Circle". You can find explanations of it in his very famous TED Talk or his book *Start with Why*. The basic idea is simple: instead of starting with what you do (as a person or especially an organization) then moving to how you get there and maybe getting to why, you should start with why. All three elements—why, how, and what—are crucial to success, but the order we approach them matters. Sinek argues that we should always start with why we are doing something in the first place, then move to how we do what we do, and finally what the end product (the what) is. By starting with why, we set ourselves up for long term success because we have started with the most important part. In effect we get the solid foundation that can create a structure that is at once strong and flexible. We have found this to be true. The reality is that while cities face the same kinds of issues, the way those issues show up can be radically different even if the cities are right next door to one another.

In the next three chapters we are going to look at the foundational principles that have led to the success of Love Our Cities through the lens of Sinek's Golden Circle.

Chapter 4: *Why Should I Care?*

Chapter 5: *How Should I Care?*

Chapter 6: *What Does Caring Look Like?*

Why Should I Care?

*"Love is the greatest power for the transformation of reality
because it pulls down the walls of selfishness and fills the ditches
that keep us apart."*

— Pope Francis

It seems like such a silly question really. If you are at all like us, your response is probably "what do you mean why should I care?" It seems like a pretty self-evident thing that we should care about others. For most of us, most of the time, it is enough to care. Of course that caveat shows where the trouble is. "Most of". What about the others—could they be convinced? What about the times that even we, those of us who really do care, get tired, burnt out and ready to throw in the towel?

The truth is, if there isn't a solid foundation—a solid reason why—then even the best of us with even the best of intentions are going to fall short. And we run the real risk that we will stop caring. It's not hard to become jaded and head in the opposite direction altogether. You can end up despising what once drove you or simply not care anymore.

Love Modesto and Love Our Cities started as part of a church. That ought to be a bit of a clue as to why we do this. Look, let's just lay some cards on the table here. Like Jeff mentioned earlier, we believe that when Jesus comes to town things should get better. We believe and are trying to follow the ethic of Jesus in what we do. We don't apologize for that. We're also not trying to beat people over the head with the Bible. We aren't saying that everyone we work with has to agree with us. That's not who we are or what we're about. We know full-well that lots and lots of people aren't going to agree with us on everything. We have partners and friends who cross all kinds of boundaries and lines.

You don't have to believe what we believe to make a difference in your city. We've seen that in lots and lots of places. You don't even have to have the same foundation we do, but we think that without it the long-term sustainability and impact is going to be limited. We also think that if you are reading this you should know where we are coming from.

We believe that what Jesus said is true, not just for some spiritual realm in the hereafter, not just for private belief, but for here and now in the world we all live in. That means we look to his teaching to ground what we do. If you take a look at our website, you are not going to find "Jesus" in blinking neon lights. You will see our vision: To love our cities so that our cities will thrive.

We know what Jesus thought was important by looking at the record of what he said and did. If you are familiar with the Bible, it's our guess that you know what we are talking about and where to look. If you're not familiar, we suggest you start with the four Gospels, or accounts, of his life—Matthew, Mark, Luke, and John[8]. Even a quick look tells us what is important to Jesus. Jesus taught his followers that they should be known by their love. That message alone tells us something about our motivations. It tells us about the way we ought to live in the world.

---

8   And if you want an even more to the point look, check out the Sermon on the Mount in Matthew 5-7 and Jesus' teaching on the greatest commandment (love God and love your neighbor) in Mark 12: 28-34.

This isn't a sermon or a Bible study. It's not a book of theology or a primer on spiritual growth. There are plenty of other books you can find that do that job, so we won't belabor the point other than to point out what one of Jesus' inner circle, the apostle John, wrote: "love means living in the way God commanded us to live. As you have heard from the beginning, his command is this: live a life of love," (2 John 6 NCV).

The longer we have done this and the more we have thought about it, the more convinced we are that there are two foundational elements to loving our neighbor. There are two ingredients, if you will, that need to be present or there are going to be problems. We aren't entirely sure we want to say that these are two sides of a single coin, but it's pretty close.

The two ingredients? Compassion and humility. We have found that the combination of compassion and humility are the core character traits, the foundation, that everything else is built on. They are at the heart of Jesus' ethic.

Compassion

What is compassion? Lots of people talk about it. Lots of people tell us we need to have compassion, to be compassionate. Lots of people complain that we aren't compassionate enough. But what do we mean? All too often when people say they have compassion, what they really mean is "I feel sorry for . . .," fill in the blank. It's easy to see the story on the news or hear about some situation on our social media feeds and feel sorry for people. We look at the devastation of an earthquake or the latest shooting or maybe even the latest commercial with miserable looking cats and dogs and Sarah McLachlan singing and we feel bad. Genuinely bad. This isn't fake. But what do we do about it

We tend to think of hatred being the opposite of compassion. In a certain sense this is true, and while social media seems to dial the hatred in people up to 11, most people in most real-life situations aren't spewing hate at every step. Yes, there are people like that and yes, we all have a tendency to "other" people who are outside of our circles, but for most there is a much bigger problem, in many ways a worse problem: apathy. Hatred can be confronted and refuted. Apathy is a much harder nut to crack.

Compassion means more than feeling bad about something. It means caring enough to do something. Over and over again when Jesus is confronted by the needs of the people who come to him, we are told he has compassion on them. And then he does something. He reaches out and heals. He cares enough to do. That is what compassion means.

So often we miss this. The thing that has made our city-wide volunteer day so important to what we do is that it helps to build compassion within people. We know full well that there are people who volunteer so that they can feel good about themselves or so that they can be seen to care or any of a host of reasons that are at heart selfish. We also know that being exposed to the real needs of real people instills real compassion—even in people who volunteered for the wrong reasons.

It is so easy to become detached from the people around us, from our neighbors, much less the people we vaguely hear about on the news or don't ever see in our day to day lives. We get up in the morning, back out of the garage, drive to work, park in the company parking lot, engage superficially with the people we work with and the barista at the local Starbucks or the waitress at the diner, we drive home, pull into our garage, close the door behind us and walk into our homes, barely even recognizing the realities of the city we live in. We don't even know our neighbors let alone the person in crisis on the other side of town.

We have heard story after story of people who volunteered and came face to face with real people in need. They went from feeling bad about the situation or wanting to feel like they had done something good to seeing people as people who mattered, people who were not so different than they were. I had friends who after participating in one of our volunteer days said "Holy cow, I had no idea. This family is unbelievable. The most beautiful people. But they're from a different ethnic background. I would never have been friends with them, but now I'm friends with them because I met them and got to know them."

Compassion sees people as intrinsically valuable enough to step out and do something. To actually see the "other" as being worthy of dignity and respect. Bob Pierce, who started the relief organization World Vision, is famous for saying "let my heart be broken by the things that break the heart of God." Pierce understood that those "things" start with people, it's why World Vision does what it does. That same heartbeat, we believe, has to lie at the heart of what we do. Every organization, every city, that we work with has a slightly different mission or cause they are working toward. It doesn't matter if they are building houses or helping to feed the homeless or providing foster homes to kids or perhaps even something that seems as small as going to talk to someone at a nursing home, somewhere in there is compassion. The way it works itself out may be different, but it is the animating force that drives us to help others.

But compassion alone is not enough. We also need to have humility.

Humility

Humility is not exactly high on the list of American traits. We are taught that if you want to make it anywhere in life you have to toot your own horn, you have to "fake it 'til you make it", and all of the other clichés and subtle pressures that tell us being humble doesn't get the job done. We get it. We are about doing, about seeing a situation, a problem and stepping up to help out. For people who are doers, problem solvers, people who see real problems and want to help (and you are probably like that if you are reading this), slowing down to ask questions is hard. You see a problem and want to fix it.

The problem is that it usually doesn't work. In our experience it hasn't been successful. It's way more successful, when we go to the community and get buy-in, when we don't think our answers are right all the time. Humility means we go and just listen and ask questions. Humility means taking the time to really assess the situation. To see if what you think is true is *actually* true. Maybe you are right, but maybe you aren't. Maybe there are other factors at play that you haven't considered. (We can virtually guarantee that is true). That kind of humility is what we are talking about.

How we approach the situation, the people in government or non-profits like relief agencies or whomever matters. It's the difference between "Hey, you've got a problem, we can fix it!" and "Hey, we're here; How can we help?" One approach is off-putting at best because it is full of pride, the other is genuinely humble. Pride says I know the *real* issue and how to fix it. Humility means listening and learning, looking beyond the obvious and the measurable. Pride parachutes in to save the day and say "look what I've done"; humility recognizes that we are here to help not to run the show, not here to relieve guilt or check a box about doing something good.

Yes, it is entirely possible that there are significant gaps in what is being done, that things are falling through the cracks and perhaps even that you see a way forward that others don't see. Great. But chances are someone else has seen the problems and the possibilities as well, and what you don't see are the hurdles they have to overcome to address the problem. The more we have a humble spirit, the more we are willing to listen and learn, to come alongside, the more we will actually understand and the more we will actually be able to help. Humility breaks down barriers, opens communication lines and sets us up to truly help. To show why compassion matters to us in the first place.

You Can't Have One Without the Other

Here's the thing, it is really, really possible to have compassion and at the same time totally miss the point because you don't have any humility. The story of the Love Our Neighbors Event vs National Night Out? That's what happens when you have compassion but not humility. It's also possible to have humility but not compassion.

As we talked through the development of this chapter, about how compassion and humility go together, and how their opposites are apathy and pride respectively, Eric developed a framework to see what's motivating us. Think of it as a heart check.

If the compassion and humility have opposites in apathy and pride, that means there are four possible combinations that we can have. Laid out on an X Y Axis, it looks like this:

From the list it is pretty obvious that there are three problematic combinations and one positive one. The list is pretty much arranged from worst to best case scenario. We can quibble over whether the second or third option is actually worse, but it seems about right to us. Let's take them one at a time, starting in the top left quadrant and moving counterclockwise:

The Social Media Diva: Apathy + Pride

We've all seen this combo and it isn't pretty. This is pretty much social media at its absolute worst. It's the complaining, shaming, condescending screeds that we see on Twitter or Facebook. It is the person who has something to say about everything and they are never kind, even if they happen to be right. They like to complain about situations but never do anything to help.

Apathy doesn't really care about situations or people at all because it doesn't affect me. Combine it with pride, feeling like we are better than the other, and well, it is particularly toxic to our communities and really to our own souls. It's deadly really. It allows us to think of "them", whoever "they" are, as simply a problem, a number. Bob the ragged homeless guy on the street becomes one of 1,500 homeless in our community. A growing problem. If we could just get rid of him, if the government would just do their jobs and fix this, or better, if we would stop enabling people like this and force them to get jobs . . ..

You see the problem? This combination instinctively and instantly, without conscious thought, dehumanizes people. It turns them into things. It puts up barriers and distance between "us" and "them". We can easily be tempted to do this in lots of ways with lots of groups of people, people who aren't us or like us. The problem is that this is the very attitude that keeps us from seeing what is actually there, from making the situation better.

Eeyore: Apathy + Humility

This is a trickier one because it often doesn't look like a problem on the surface. It may not be as bad as apathy and pride, but the combination is actually not so different. This person isn't likely to create a tweet storm about how bad "they" are. They might not ever say anything at all. If they do, it's generally not going to be inflammatory. In some ways, though, it is even more insidious. This is the person probably genuinely feels sorry for the homeless, but they couldn't pick Bob out of a lineup even if they saw him every day. Instead, they see an overwhelming problem and feel that there is absolutely nothing that they can do to help.

The combination of apathy and humility still reduces people to things, it just puts a more sympathetic face on it. Subtly and over time it twists genuine humility into a sort of negative pride. Genuine humility realizes that I may not have all the answers, this kind of twisted humility says, "I am worthless and can do nothing." When apathy and humility come together in this form indecision and inertia set in. Nothing gets done because nothing gets started.

Unfortunately, a great many people live in this space. They see the reality of the problems around them but feel so overwhelmed and unable or unequipped to address the problem that they don't even try. They aren't connected to actual people living in crisis or they are so busy with the concerns of their own lives that they don't stop to think about others as real people.

Bull in a China Shop: Compassion + Pride

Most of us have met this guy too. He's a force of nature. You gotta love his enthusiasm, you know that he actually does care and has some decent ideas. But you can only take so much of him because he is going to wear you out. Heaven forbid you have ideas of your own that might not exactly line up with his. We all know that isn't going to work. When people like this lead, the people around him stop talking, stop offering solutions and pretty soon just stop showing up. Sheer force of personality may keep things going, keep attracting new people to the mission, but pretty soon they are going to burn people out or push them away and the carousel keeps turning.

The opposite problem of the last combination is the well-intentioned person who has all the answers to all the problems, and they are out to change the world and tell you about it. There is actual concern here. Real recognition that there are issues and problems in the real world. Unfortunately, this person also generally believes that everyone else is probably undereducated, unenlightened, or just plain incompetent. If they were put in charge, *then* things would be better. And they would be better yesterday.

This guy sees Bob living on the street, pushing a cart and knows what to do. He has the solution to all of Bob's problems. Of course, he likely didn't bother to ask Bob his name, didn't think to ask Bob about how he got to this place, and he isn't looking for details. Bob, you have to get a job. You have to clean yourself up and decide to try harder. Come with me . . . and Bob has become a project. Success, well, Bob becomes a trophy. A picture on the wall or a story told over and over—a poster child and no longer a real person if he ever was one.

Love in Action: Compassion + Humility

Genuine concern that moves us to do something in a way that actively loves others. Together compassion and humility lead us to see others as real people, to decide that we are actually going to help and then compels us to learn what the realities of the situation are so that we can actually do some good.

Together compassion and humility lead us to see Bob, to ask his name and to treat him with dignity and respect as a human being. To show up with more than a handout, but also with a desire to know who he is and what matters to him. What are his hopes and dreams? How did he get here? This is not a parachute in and "fix the problem" approach. This is a spend enough time and energy to earn Bob's trust, to learn who he is, approach. Genuine compassion and humility will stick around long enough to find out that Bob taught at Stanford. His wife left him. He got depressed, so depressed in fact, that he just stopped living his life. Together compassion and humility recognize Bob as a person, walk beside him and reach out a hand to help.

The thing about bringing compassion and humility together is that they work together to create balance. The person who has compassion and humility doesn't think that they can do everything. This person recognizes that they have value and so does the other. They can't do everything, but they can do something. And they do.

Reality Check:

Let's be real. No one is completely any one of these four. People aren't formulas (which is kind of the point) but formulas can help us think through things, assess ourselves and get better. Truth be told we all have blind spots. We all have areas in our lives where we are apathetic, where we are prideful. Even on our best days, in the best versions of ourselves we stumble and screw up, we get it wrong.

The truth of matter is that we all get it wrong a lot. We have made lots of mistakes with Love Modesto and Love Our Cities over the years. We have listened or understood the issues faced by the agencies doing the work or we thought that our pet project was the really big need when in fact it was something else. But we are learning. We have made it a point to see people as people, to have humble spirits even when we don't naturally—to listen and learn, to ask questions. We still don't always get it right, but we are getting better. The more cities that we help, the more people that come alongside, the more we get to see and hear about people actually making a difference. We get to help others and in turn they help us. We end up being much better together.

Compassion and humility together are what real love looks like. In Eric's Ted Talk, he says the definition of love is sacrificing oneself for the spiritual growth of another. That's the foundation of what we do. We can't stress it enough. If both elements aren't there, well you will either never get started or it won't last.

So, how's your heart?

City Spotlight:
New Braunfels, Texas

Year Joined: 2019
City Leader: Kim Francis

Tell us a bit about your city:

New Braunfels is a vacation town nestled halfway between Austin and San Antonio. 20 years ago, New Braunfels was a sleepy vacation town of 36,000. In 2019 we were located in the second fastest growing county in the nation bursting at over 90,000 citizens. Most Texans know us for our rivers (Comal and Guadalupe—great for tubing in the hot Texas summers), German festivals (Wurstfest or Wassailfest anyone?) and small-town feel. We are notably famous for our high-school mascot-the Unicorn, the oldest dance hall and bakery in Texas (Gruene Hall and Naegelin's), the largest gas station in the world (Buc-ee's), the world's best waterpark (Schlitterbahn), and Charlie Duke, Apollo 16's moon walking astronaut. Founded in 1845 by Prince Solms of Braunfels, Germany, New Braunfelers love celebrating our heritage. It's not uncommon to hear accordion players holler "Prost!" while you're watching a beer stein-holding contest in our German-influenced restaurants.

What are some of the unique challenges you face?

As a destination city that has experienced steady, rapid growth, social needs and resources have fallen prey to the public infrastructure needed to accommodate more residents and our strong tourist economy. Most residents and especially vacationers don't want to hear about the trials of the homeless or hunger pangs of the impoverished, so in the past, these issues have been neglected. But with a bursting population, the problems are harder to ignore. These problems are not necessarily unique to our community, they are experienced by many across the country. Housing prices increased faster than wages and it has become difficult for many lifelong New Braunfels residents to stay in the town they have always called home. Our suicide rate has crept higher than that of the State of Texas for both adults and kids due to a lack of mental health and substance abuse recovery resources. It seems we cannot give away enough healthy food to keep those most vulnerable nourished. We have no public transportation system or homeless shelter, and skill-based vocational training is difficult to access.

How did you hear about Love Our Cities and how has Love Our Cities helped you?

A resident of Denver for a decade, I had connections in Colorado who told me about Corrie at COS I Love You, the Love Our Cities organization in Colorado Springs. Corrie's organization was years down the road from where we were, and she graciously gave us some pointers and advice on our next steps in our journey. They were having great success connecting needs and resources in her city and put us in touch with Eric at Love Our Cities to help us with Big Serve, our annual volunteer day and our big vision to further help our city.

Knowing there was a group of like-minded individuals across the country working on unifying and serving their cities was a huge boost for us. When we found Love Our Cities, we felt like we weren't alone, that there was a team of leaders on the same adventure in their cities. Trying to blaze a new trail of service and unity in your city is slow and full of roadblocks. Journeying with others and hearing their successes, frustrations, and encouragement makes all the difference! Our volunteer days had grown from 25 volunteers to closer to 500 people and we knew we had to streamline our activities or we'd get overwhelmed in the details. Within weeks of talking with Eric, we felt like the road was going to be easier because we were linking arms with Love Our Cities. Eric called me often, learned our story, and guided us toward creating our online volunteer portal.

The Zoom calls with other Love Our Cities leaders helped us see that we were doing some things well and provided ideas for how we could serve our city more effectively. In 2020, we talked about handling volunteer days with COVID and had discussions about what each city was doing to address racial tensions. Our faith-based Serve Spot team talks about John 17 and Isaiah 58 at just about every meeting we have. Jesus said in John 17:23 "I in them and you in me—so that they may be brought to complete unity. Then the world will know that you sent me and have loved them even as you have loved me." Our goal is to unite the Church so that the world may see that Jesus loves every citizen in our community. Isaiah 58 is God's words to his people telling them that he wants them to share their food with the hungry, give shelter to the homeless, and remove the chains that bind people. Then (after you've done these things), God says, your light will shine out from the darkness and the darkness around you will be as bright as noon. Isn't that what we're after? Bright lights of hope shining on every city in our world? Love Our Cities is doing both of these things: unifying and serving well and encouraging others to do the same.

Tell us about your city-wide volunteer day and other efforts you have undertaken:
Since its inception in 2014, Big Serve, our volunteer day, has grown from a quarterly Sunday morning event with a few dozen volunteers from one congregation to an annual weekend event with hundreds of volunteers from a dozen congregations.

We tell our volunteers to "be the Church, don't just attend one." Big Serve is our introduction, for many, to service and nonprofits in our area. It's an "on ramp" to giving and serving. We recognize that painting a wall or stocking a shelf alone won't change the world but painting next to a stranger and sharing your stories might plant a seed. Knowing hundreds of others are doing work around your community can encourage you to do more. Coming back year after year to dozens of nonprofits and serving with excellence reminds them that the Church is here and there are folks who care.

The Church used to be the central guiding force of a community. In 2020, this is no longer the case. The Church has to be creative in how we share the Gospel and at Serve Spot, we feel serving in unity is a way for us to gain a voice with our neighbors and love them as Jesus does. We want to show New Braunfels what we are for (love, uplifting others, compassion, giving our lives away, helping our neighbors) rather than what we're against. Big Serve Weekend is one of our ways to give a unified message of hope and Jesus' love to New Braunfels.

In 2019, a dozen pastors saw that Big Serve alone wasn't enough. With the rate of growth in New Braunfels, we knew there were other ways to effectively serve our community and so we stepped out of our silos and began monthly meetings to figure out how to serve our city better together. We talked to community experts about statistics on housing, food insecurity, and crime. We met with other community leaders around the country to learn best practices, we asked our local nonprofits what they felt we could do to help out. From there, www.servespot.org was born. We have information about all of our local nonprofits and other nearby resources; Love Our Cities helped us to add the volunteer portal. We also now have a local Nonprofit Job Board and other resources for faith leaders who want to dig deeper into service. We are growing into the "spot" in town where we can help connect needs and people.

What others are saying:
"New Braunfels is a city that loves neighbors well. Our family has witnessed it when we suffered tragic loss, and we too have been able to give back and bless others through Big Serve. Thankful that churches have come together to unite in serving. Because we can do more for others together."

"Big Serve has helped open my eyes to ministries around town that I didn't know existed. After serving there once, I find myself reaching out to them throughout the year by either donating, serving, or recommending their services to those in need."

"I love watching the Church work together in unity to love our city well!"

"Big Serve was the launching point for us to recognize that we can do more good together. I'm so thankful for the relationships I've built with other pastors through Big Serve!"

"This is amazing. I can picture our Lord smiling as He sees His bride working in unity and being his hands."

"During Big Serve a boy and his family chose to serve with me at the Homeless Mat Project. He learned the steps to make a plastic mat for the homeless. What he seemed to enjoy most was learning how to crochet the mat. He was very proud of his accomplishment. While doing this, he remarked, 'When my family was on the street, we could have used one of these.' This moment has inspired me to continue the ministry and reminded me that everyone has the ability to serve."

How Do I Care?

*"Compassion is an emotional upheaval in your gut that says this
is not right. This has to change."*

— Walter Brueggemann

In some ways asking why we should care is the easy part. At some
level we know it. We may not have it all figured out, we may get it
wrong in places, but chances are there isn't a whole lot about why we
should care that is shocking or completely new. If anything, the last chapter should have clarified things for you that you probably already sensed
on some level. Hopefully it gave you some handles for sharing why we
should care.

How we should care is another story.

Here's where we tend to look for techniques. We want to develop skills
to produce a product. It is the way we are taught to think. It is the way that
we are taught to approach life. You want to read, well, here's the strategy.
You want to learn to speak another language, here's the foolproof program.

Here's the thing, there is no foolproof program for how. There is no magic formula. There's a simple choice. It's a choice that we all make every day in lots of ways and in lots of areas of life.

Do we collaborate or do we go it alone? Do we work together or in silos? For decades, the ideal of the American hero—the entrepreneur, the cowboy, the action hero, and many others—was the lone guy who by his own grit and determination triumphed against the odds. Going it alone is built into our very culture. While it is increasingly true that younger generations think more collaboratively, the question remains. Even if you are more inclined to work in groups or share responsibilities, relying on others involves risk.

The Big Choice: Silos or Collaboration

When it comes to working for the betterment of our communities, the choice between silos or collaboration will show up in lots of ways and it will show up early on. This really isn't a question of personality or style. It's not a "well my generation does it this way and yours does it that way" kind of a thing. It's more basic than that on one level and it transcends it on another. It's a question of effectiveness and scope, of time commitment and impact.

Silos or collaboration.

The choice is almost perfectly illustrated by a situation we faced in Modesto. Like many communities in California, homelessness is a serious problem for Modesto. There are two large organizations and many small ones trying to tackle this problem in our city. The two larger organizations have existed for decades and grew significantly on their own. During the first few years of Love Modesto, I (Jeff) talked to these organizations quite a bit. But I realized something: they almost never talked to one another.

So I called a lunch meeting for the leaders of all of these organizations—big and small. Some I knew well; some I didn't know at all. Almost all of them came. That lunch meeting birthed an ongoing monthly meeting to hear about the successes being seen and to understand where they were duplicating services as well as where the gaps were. Eventually, I stepped out of the way and they continued to meet. New, sustainable efforts to deal with the complex problems surrounding homelessness in our area were launched. To this day, those efforts bring these different organizations together to work on the homeless problem.

They didn't even realize that they had chosen to be siloed and it was hampering their efforts until someone showed them what collaboration could do.

Silos

The word "Silos" has become something of a buzzword in the business world. Generally, it means that one group or division within a company has little interaction with or even knowledge of what another part of the company does. It's understandable when this happens in a big company and there are groups and divisions who may well exist or function in very different markets or even industries. But it happens in smaller businesses as well.

Silos can serve a legitimate function. There are some very real advantages to silos. Silos are generally smaller; they are easier to shape and direct. In a word, silos offer control. If you are an artist or craftsman, if you are a writer or have a very niche market you are filling in business, a silo might not be a bad thing. Silos allow for quality control and, if you have the skills, they can also allow you to ensure that your vision and goals are met. Those are not insignificant things.

At the same time, the strengths of a silo are also the things that create its limitations. The more control you can or do exercise, the more constraints that you are also imposing. This means, of course, that you will necessarily be limiting the scale and the effect that you can have. You may be a very high-capacity person and you may devote your entire waking moments to whatever cause or business or interest you have, but you will always be the limiting factor if you are going it alone.

There is a second limitation to creating silos that we often overlook, namely the higher chance of unintended negative consequences. When you work alone or in a very small group you are just going to have less access to information or resources that might be crucial to successfully meeting your goals. The consequences for a painter choosing a paint color that has gone out of style might be minimal. The consequences for the company creating tubes of artist quality paints of that same color might be far more costly.

When it comes to helping our communities, the advantage of a silo is that you can probably get something off the ground pretty quickly if you have the time, willpower and resources. The disadvantage is that, unless you have unlimited resources (and let's face it, we don't) your footprint won't be that big and you may well end up running afoul of local ordinances or duplicate programs. Worst case, you make the problem that you were trying to solve worse because you aren't taking something important into account, something that others might know.

Collaboration

If you are a Millennial or younger, chances are collaboration is in your DNA. You grew up working in groups in school, you are practically conditioned toward collaboration and against competition. There are some serious and probably obvious advantages to collaboration. Realistically the capacity for larger impact immediately gets bigger when you have more people at the table. You have more access to more information and more resources. Increased information and resources can lead to a more holistic approach to solving problems. Notice we said *can* lead, it's not automatic, you have to work at it.

When we are willing to collaborate with others there is a much better chance of increasing overall engagement and influence. There are a hundred different clichés that we could include here:

The sum is greater than the parts

It's not what you know it's who you know

Stop, collaborate and listen

The list goes on. They are clichés for a reason. They point to something true. Collaboration leads to increased impact.

But it's a double-edged sword. Increased engagement means that you get to influence others, but it also means that they get to influence you.

It really is double-edged. You may well be able to influence others, help them to see things that they may not see, perhaps even bring them to your point of view. But it works both ways. They will influence you as well. There is just no way around it. This can be a good thing and it can be a bad thing. All of us have room for growth. All of us need to be challenged and to be open to seeing things from different perspectives, to learn.

At the same time, if you aren't careful, you can get off track from what you are trying to accomplish. Sometimes we need this because we were headed in the wrong direction. We have had cases where we thought that we had the right idea or saw a significant problem that was not being addressed, but when we dug in further, we found out that really wasn't the thing that was the most pressing or that it was a symptom of a larger issue. When that happens, we adjust because the ultimate goal is the same. The tricky part is making sure that there isn't significant mission drift.

There's another thing about collaboration that we have to acknowledge. Collaboration, real collaboration, takes time. It's messy, inefficient. Collaboration means that we have to sit down together, we have to bring others to the table and give them a real voice. It means that we are going to have to go in, eyes open, and realize that we are not going to agree with everyone that we are sitting with on every (and maybe even lots) of issues.

At the end of the day, there is no question that collaboration will take more effort, more time, more of you. But we believe it is worth it. It's worth it because the people we collaborate with are people who deserve compassion and humility too. It's worth it because if we actually believe in what we say we believe then we will live it out both with people who we agree with and the ones we don't agree with. If we really believe that people are intrinsically valuable and deserve dignity and respect, that we should be making things better, then well, we are going to have to collaborate in order to be effective. Over 10 years in, we are seeing the real fruit of this approach. Yes, it can take more effort to overcome inertia at the beginning. Yes, it takes a lot of effort. But once things are moving? Well, the dividends can be amazing.

Let's be real. Collaboration can be scary. It means crossing lines that you might not want to cross. We're not talking about core belief lines here. But lines, nonetheless. In faith communities that might mean coming together across denominations or faiths to accomplish a mutual goal. It doesn't mean everyone agrees, and to be sure there will have to be lines that aren't crossed no matter who you are. Boundaries will have to be set. But what happens when a church partners with a school to tutor kids who need it? What happens when the foster care agency says to the church that they need families to step up? What happens when government leaders let non-profits and faith communities know where they are struggling and need help? Of course, there are real limits and boundaries, there are rules that have to be followed. But that doesn't mean collaboration can't happen. It can. We have seen it.

So, if real collaboration takes energy and effort, if it is truly the way to make things different in our towns, what does it look like?

Glad you asked.

The Foundation of Collaboration.

How do we care? Two words:

Relationships.

Trust.

That's it. Just like compassion and humility, they go together. Simple, but not easy. In fact, it may well be hard. It's definitely going to be messy because people are messy. You are messy and so am I. We all have rough edges and blind spots. We all have those areas of life that we aren't proud of; the weak areas and places where no matter how hard we try we remain selfish and small. But the truth is, no matter how much we are messed up we all need relationships, we all need trust.

Relationships

Almost 400 years ago the Scottish poet John Donne wrote the famous line "no man is an island". No matter who we are or what our background, young or old, rich or poor, introvert or extrovert, or any of a hundred other qualifiers, we all need relationships. We all have relationships. Some of us are better at developing relationships than others, but none of us are islands.

Relationships seem to come easy to some of us and for others they seem anything but easy. The truth of the matter is that no relationship of significance is completely easy and sometimes it's tough even for those of us who have an easier time of it. I (Jeff) am a connector. I love meeting new people; I love being with people. Not everyone is like that, but even for me relationships can be hard. Sometimes they don't work the way I would like. When my kids were small my wife and I wanted to help out in their school. We wanted to come alongside the principal to help out at the school. She wasn't interested—you're the parent, I am the principal, stay in your lane. That was a hard pill to swallow. We just wanted to help. Relationships don't always work.

But they are necessary.

Relationships have to be built. They rarely "just happen". They take time and effort. They require presence. For the first ten years I was a pastor in Modesto, most of the relationships I had were with the college students that I worked with and what I sometimes call "church world". Very early on, I am pretty sure I was still an intern at Big Valley, I met Marvin Jacobo. Marvin was one of the longest serving youth pastors in town and was one of the primary organizers of a group of local pastors. Very quickly he became one of the most important mentors I have ever had (so important that I asked him to be one of the founding board members when we started our own non-profit). To this day, Marvin's example, especially when it comes to building relationships, is remarkable. He models what building relationships ought to mean.

When you are trying to build something, whether it's a business or a ministry, a relief organization or even something like Love Modesto it can be very tempting to think of relationships as networking, a localized version of LinkedIn. Marvin has shown me over and over again that that is not what building relationships means. No one is going to deny that knowing the right people is important, but a relationship is way more than that.

Networking says "what can I get from you? How can I leverage the fact that I know you?" Relationships aren't about a transaction; they are about people. Relationships say, "Tell me who you are, I want to know you for you, not for what I get out of knowing you." If our foundation really is compassion and humility, then that isn't simply reserved for people we help. It has to extend to the people we work with.

When I transitioned from college pastor to outreach pastor and then started Love Modesto, I didn't really know any of the "players" in town outside of church world. I didn't know who was leading the nonprofits doing relief work or the heads of city and county agencies. I had to intentionally seek out those people. I started with the people I knew, with the guy from Habitat for Humanity who went to my church, with my wife's connections as a social worker. I asked questions and learned who they knew and who they thought I should get in touch with. Slowly, overtime, I built relationships with people in all kinds of positions and together we have built something important, something that matters to our city.

But if I had simply tried to network with the "right people", even by way connecting through people I already knew, it never would have worked. People know when you are trying to use them. None of us like to be used. Real relationships require trust. I like how Eric talks about the way we can't separate relationships from trust.

Trust

I (Eric) can't stress enough how much trust and relationships go together. We could almost say they have to be trusting relationships. Here's what I mean, I've seen a consistent pattern play out in our community. On a pragmatic level, Love Modesto is now at a place where we're dealing with the heads of a lot of different organizations. And the common ground is that we're trying to address these issues in our community, but really, I care just as much about the executive director of a given group or agency, as a person, not just because of his or her position. That's what it means to have not just a relationship, but trust.

As leaders who are trying to work together to accomplish something in our community, as we build genuine relationships, we have come to care about the people that we're working with as much as the organizations and the causes of our work. Because when you get on the same page it's not just that we're coming together for this common cause. We need each other and someone else's personal story and their success and their wellbeing matters to me just as much now as the cause that we're trying to affect. Because if they go down, their organization's going to go down, our community goes down. It's not just caring about the outcome; it's caring about the person. So now if I'm meeting with Francine over coffee and all of a sudden Kathy who's the head of one of the government agencies in town walks in and sits down. They're board members and best friends and Kathy sees that we not only know but actually care about Francine and now we're all talking, and a new connection is born. Collaboration expands.

But again, it's not about expanding your contact list even though you actually do need to do that. It's about actually caring about that person as a person. Asking, "How are you doing? You're getting married? When? Tell me about what's going on." It's about sharing pictures of kids and talking about life and being in that person's corner.

Jeff talks about the influence Marvin has had on him, and I think one of the things that we have both really appreciated about him is that he lives this idea out. He has really reminded us that the higher up in leadership people get, whether in business or government or church leadership or whatever, the fewer true friends that you actually have. People are always coming to you wanting something from you. So when we come alongside someone and treat them well, when we care about the politician that we don't agree with and make it a point not to talk about them or to betray a confidence, we build trust. We show that we care about them as people and in the end, guess what, we also get more done.

I think a lot of people in the circles that we run with are figuring this out and doing this well. City engagement leaders we are working with understand collaboration, they understand its importance and they get that it requires trust and relationships. Yeah. It's harder and it's slower. But once you figure those things out, the fruit that that produces is amazing. I should really say this is slower and harder up front, but it builds a much bigger flywheel that can produce much larger results.

Hey, it's Jeff again. We keep repeating the "slower and harder" thing for a reason. Trust takes time. You don't trust someone who just shows up out of the blue. Proof matters. I asked Marvin about why this is so important and here's what he said.

"Nothing in our city gets done without trust and relationships. The most precious currency we have is trust. If you are not trusted or your organization is not trusted, it will get around. Having the trust of people is huge. It means you are tight on accounting your money, you don't make promises you can't keep. You don't talk— you don't gossip. In this generation especially, the source of the message is just as important as the message. You have to listen and really, really hear people. I don't pass judgment or give my opinion.

Cultures do it differently, so I do my homework about different cultures. I spend a lot more time asking questions than making pronouncements. I was told, especially in groups that I don't know 'show up, shut up, and don't speak until you're asked.' Sometimes we feel like we have the right to just make pronouncements, but we need to really listen. We need to slow down and listen because there are a lot of people who don't trust, they are afraid of being pimped out. They have been pimped out.

I let people know that I want to be their friend. Eventually through the friendship I will benefit, and they will benefit from me. I listen to who is in the know, who carries weight. I want to meet them, to know them. I don't ask for anything. People know if you really love them. They really know. This is different than just 'closing the deal.'"[9]

---

9   Jacobo, Marvin. Interview with Jeff Pishney. Personal interview. Modesto, CA, August 6, 2019.

I think you can see why we pay attention to what Marvin says.

Is there a risk to building these kinds of relationships? Sure. It's going to eat time. It just is. But what do you get in return? Yes, you are going to have to be more vulnerable, more real. But you are going to become a better person because of the connections you make. Your life will be enriched. You will be exposed to lots of people who are different from you and you will see that they are not statistics or "one of those" but they are real people. And because of these relationships your impact will be bigger. Here's another aspect that you may not have thought about. If you don't show up, if you don't care enough to learn about who is doing what in your city, you will never get a hearing for what you want to do. Bottom line: if you don't show yourself to be trustworthy you simply won't get heard. That means you have to put in the time and effort. You have to prove that you are trustworthy. When you do that, you will have earned the right to be heard. The reason why Love Modesto has been so successful for so long is that we have proved who we are and what we are about. We have proved that we care about the people we want to help *and* the people who want to help them. We have shown that we can follow the rules and we will do what we say we are going to do. We have built trusting relationships with the business community and the non-profits in town, with the schools and city government from the public works department to the fire and police departments and DCFS and the list goes on. We work across denominational lines and even across faith lines. We know this works. We know that we are trusted, and we have learned how to work across all kinds of lines. We have become friends with lots of people along the way and that alone has been worth the effort.

But What About . . .?

I can hear the questions, the worry. We get it. We have been there and have heard and had many of the same ones. What if I care about this and really want it to happen but I am an introvert? What about people we disagree with? How do we partner with _____? What about rules and boundaries? What about separation of church and state?

First, take a breath. Yes, there are real issues and real hurdles and yes, you will need to think through what those things look like. Second, let me repeat, we have been there and there really are ways forward. We have said it over and over, Love Modesto was birthed in a church. Yes, we had to deal with concerns about church and state issues. Yes, we worked with a bunch of churches who were not on the same page as us. I could go on and on. One of the beauties of being part of a network like Love Our Cities is that the cities who come on board with us get access to more than just what we have learned, they also get access to what other cities have learned, they get to hear how others have navigated these same waters. We have learned a lot from them. There are a lot of different questions we hear raised, but they basically break down into three kinds: personality questions, boundary questions, and what we call "sector" questions.

Personality questions usually start like this: Do I have to be an extravert to start something like Love Modesto in my town? No. Absolutely, positively not. I won't lie, if you are an extravert, it will be easier because you are energized by people. But introverts can do this too. If you love people and are willing to put in the effort you can do it. But here's a secret that we will talk about in more detail later—you aren't doing this alone. In fact, it's our recommendation that you *don't* do this alone. Often introverts spend more time thinking and mulling over the issues and the needs of their community, they may well see the needs more clearly or quickly than others. If that's you, find a partner who is an extravert. Someone you trust who will help you to be better at connecting with others. If you are painfully shy, well guess what, you are probably not the person to be the face of starting a movement in your city, but you may well be the person who finds the person who can be.

Boundaries are important. We are a faith-based organization. We have a faith statement for people who sign on with us. But the people we work with to get the job done? We work with lots of different groups and people. Remember my friend the atheist radio producer? Coming from the church world has made me sensitive to the very real concerns that people have about beliefs and boundaries. Truth be told, some of the totally "secular" groups we have worked with have similar concerns. A friend of ours, Jon Talbert, says it like this: "Can we be friends and not partners?" His point is simple, we can be friends and not agree on everything, we can even work on projects together and have very different beliefs. You don't have to agree on everything religiously or politically to help clean up a park or tutor kids in math or any of a hundred other projects. We are not talking about gathering together for a joint community prayer service and pretending that we all agree on everything. We can help you navigate the thorny boundary questions.

The third area of questions are "sector" questions. When we talk about sectors, we mean broad categories of society. Typically, we break things down into six broad sectors: Faith, Government, Nonprofits, Business, School, and Community (we will talk more about these in the next chapter). It's not an exhaustive list but it covers the bases pretty well. As you can imagine, the biggest questions are of the "church and state" variety and often they are coming from the state side of the ledger as much as from the faith side. Let me be real here, you have way more freedom to interact than you think. We live in California, and we haven't just made this work, we have developed real partnerships. If we can do it here, it can be done. Yes, you have to obey the rules. If you are a church, no, you cannot proselytize when you are working with schools or other governmental agencies, but you don't have to stop being who you are either.

Real collaboration will be uncomfortable at times, but it is worth the effort. When you put in the time and effort to build trusting relationships with people to achieve a common goal it is amazing what you can accomplish. When you have real friendships with people, when you respect and care about them you will find that you really can collaborate in meaningful ways. You will even find that you are willing to champion others.

City Spotlight:
Snoqualmie Valley, Washington

Year Joined: 2019
City Leader: Emily Ridout

Tell us a bit about your city:

The Snoqualmie Valley is made up of five charming small towns—Duvall, Carnation, Fall City, Snoqualmie, and North Bend—that run along the beautiful Snoqualmie River. Together the 5 towns have a population of about 34,000. Situated between Seattle and the foothills of the Cascade Mountains, including the majestic Mount Si, the Snoqualmie Valley boasts premiere outdoor activities, fertile soil for farming, spectacular sites like the Snoqualmie Falls, and rich heritage. The Snoqualmie Indian Tribe is an important part of our community and history, stewarding this land for centuries. The agricultural and timber value of the Snoqualmie Valley was discovered in the late 1800s launching the logging operations that have shaped much of the culture and history of the Snoqualmie Valley.

The Snoqualmie Valley is an incredibly special and beautiful community with hard-working and generous people. The Valley is rich with recreational activities and features special sites like Mount Si and The Snoqualmie Falls along with unique iconic businesses like Treehouse Point and the Salish Lodge. Being just 30-minutes east of Seattle, the Snoqualmie Valley has rapidly grown in the last 15 years as employees from businesses like Microsoft, Amazon, and Google seek rural communities with a relatively short commute.

What do you love about the Snoqualmie Valley, and what are some of the unique challenges you face?

The drastic growth in Snoqualmie Valley has come with its challenges as those who have called the Valley home for many generations fight to preserve the natural resources and rich heritage of the community. We also face great challenges competing for human services funding and resources with the larger densely populated communities in the eastside suburbs of Seattle. And although the valley stretches across beautiful land, the geographic range does make it hard for the valley to stay united and connected in working together on important issues and needs.

How did you hear about Love Our Cities and how has Love Our Cities helped you?

I heard about Love Our Cities through some close friends from college who live in Modesto. I followed the effort for a few years and when I moved into an outreach role at SVA Church, I knew it was time to bring that level of collaboration and unity to our community. Our connection to Love Our Cities has allowed Love Snoqualmie Valley to have a significant impact in our community in a number of ways:

Unifying Churches across the Valley: Before, Love Snoqualmie Valley churches worked in silos, often unintentionally competing against each other to serve in similar ways and meet similar needs for our community. Our leadership team is made up of 8 influential churches that have come together like a family to support each other, our churches, and the community at large. We see our collective resources going further and believe that we are operating more as one body, being The Church, instead of individual churches.

Healing old wounds: While intentions were always good, efforts launched by some churches in the valley caused wounds that continued for many years until Love Snoqualmie Valley was formed. The model of bringing churches together, without promoting one single church, or even churches themselves over other sectors, opened the door to new partnerships that had been closed for many years. A great example: we had two separate food banks operating completely independently of one another just two miles apart because of this history. Through the relationship building of Love Snoqualmie Valley, these walls came down, and now we are experiencing collaboration among these entities.

Cross-sector awareness: Love Snoqualmie Valley has served as a bridge to bring our sectors together. Our volunteer day was the first effort of its kind to actively pursue all sectors of our community working together to make it a better place. We have loved watching businesses come to know nonprofits that they want to support, churches being invited to have a voice at the local government level, and small businesses receiving new levels of support from community residents who didn't even know they existed.

Opportunity for individual engagement: We often hear that people living in the Snoqualmie Valley don't know how to engage with the community to volunteer and make a difference. Love Snoqualmie Valley opened the door for people to find an area of the community they are passionate about. What started as volunteering for a project turned into ongoing support for nonprofits, churches, and local government.

Tell us about your city-wide volunteer day and other efforts you have undertaken:

We hosted our first valley-wide volunteer day in the fall of 2019. We hoped to have 500 volunteers and ended up with almost 1,000 working on 30 projects across the Snoqualmie Valley. Due to COVID in 2020, we shifted our efforts from a volunteer day to creating an online resource platform providing a place for people to give and get help in response to the massive increase of needs. We have also hosted a Give & Go drop off donation event in August of 2020. We feel relatively young in our identity but the impact we have seen in the last two years has been phenomenal. We soon plan to become our own 501c3 and continue to serve and love our community in whatever ways are most needed.

What others are saying:
"Love SV is doing incredible work bringing our community together and serving ALL those in need. Thank you Love SV Team!"

– Lori Kissick

"Love this so much! One of the main reasons I want to move to the Valley, that awesome sense of community!"

– Cindy Vet

"Thank you Love Snoqualmie Valley for the amazing opportunity today to build community. I am so grateful to share this with my son! Let's do this again!"

– Tina Longwell

"THANK YOU for the clean-up in Fall City- it looks great."

– Jay Bluher

"What a fun day! Thank you so much for the opportunity."

– Helene Wentink

What Does Caring Look Like?

"The litmus test of our love for God is our love of neighbor."
— Brennan Manning

This is where the rubber hits the road, where all the foundations and reasons, the processes and techniques come together to actually produce something. Let's face it, we can have the best intentions in the world, we can have a plan to make things work with all the contacts and friendships that we need, but if we don't actually do anything with all that, well, what difference does it make really? Lots of people have lots of good ideas and never get anything off the ground.

Love Modesto has been actively making a difference for over a decade. Love Our Cities has learned how to replicate that success around the country. If you only look at the surface, it would be easy to think that what makes us unique is our city-wide volunteer day. After all, it is the single most visible aspect of what we do. But lots of people do volunteer days. The why and the how of what we do are vital. Together they form the foundation and the platform on which we have been able to build something successful. From there, several specific elements make Love Our Cities unique.

From Collaboration to Championing Others

It's one thing to collaborate, right? It's one thing to say, "we care and we want to help", "we want to collaborate". But we can still be compassionate and active and even work for the good of our city and partner with others and at the end of the day it is still really about our own self-fulfillment, building our program or empire or whatever. Collaborating with others is great, but it really is possible to jostle that to make it really about me. Lots of times we don't even realize we are doing it. But if you really want to know if you're about others in your community, take an inventory of who you are talking about, what you are talking about. When you find yourself championing others, that's when you know that it isn't really about you.

It feels backwards in so many ways. Everything that we have been taught in business and marketing says you have to talk about and promote what you do. When you are a nonprofit who needs money and you have to do fundraising. There's tension there. We feel it. We're trying to create and promote our own initiatives. It's easy to view the other nonprofits in town as the competition—even the ones that you know are doing good stuff and who you are friends with. We're going to promote their stuff? But there is also a freedom in doing that. There's real beauty in it. And here's the truth that a lot of times we don't like to admit to ourselves—a lot of the time, probably most of the time, those organizations know the problems and solutions to their specific cause better than we do. The mission who works with the homeless knows more about helping the homeless than I do. The foster agency may be overworked and understaffed, but they understand the needs more than I do. Habitat for Humanity knows who needs housing and how to build a house. You get the point.

Right now, we have a page on our website with over 40 donation opportunities for other organizations. We are promoting them. On our website. On purpose. Not just to sign up to volunteer for a project but to actually donate money to those organizations. From the very beginning of Love Modesto, we have thought this way. Our very first projects included things like a Habitat for Humanity project. We are still working with them today.

Here's how this works. We partner with other groups and organizations to do service projects for our city-wide volunteer day. People sign up ahead of time for the project they want to be a part of. Take Habitat for Humanity as an example. The project leader works for the local Habitat chapter. The project is his. On the day of the project, he connects with the volunteers, his organization gets the shot in the arm for what they are doing in the community, they get their project done, but it doesn't end there.

If that leader follows up well with the people that volunteered—they've got phone numbers because they have texted those volunteers with details and they have their emails, and hopefully they built relationships that day with all the people who worked together that day. If they do a good job, they're going to get far more than people who just volunteer for a day. We estimate that they get a 30% better volunteer retention if they do a good job connecting with and following up with those volunteers. The one-day event just became a way for those organizations to increase their ongoing volunteer pool. And when people love what you do and they believe in what they do, they're going to give to what you do. And so that, that leader has an opportunity to get funding as well. And it's not just nonprofits. It also works for businesses. Our local Subaru dealer has partnered with us to lead projects almost from the beginning. When the volunteers who worked with them need to get a new car, who do you think they are thinking about first?

And guess what? It's not a one-way street. They promote you too. It only makes sense. We are connecting volunteers to other organizations, not just releasing but actively recruiting all these people to go to them. How much do organizations pay for leads? It's a multimillion dollar a year business. So in the end, our partners love us because we are really helping them to do what they do. They are more than happy to return the favor when we have something we need to promote because they know that we are really helping them too.

We like to say that we are the Airbnb of community engagement. What does Airbnb do? It connects people who need lodging with places to stay. We connect causes to the community. It might be the nonprofit helping the homeless or the school that needs its playground redone or fill in the blank. We promote them and their projects. We tell them to dream big and we work to get as many people as possible to their project. And we don't charge anything. When it comes to the projects for the city-wide volunteer day, we give them training so that they are completely prepared to have the best possible event. That is what championing others looks like.

We do it locally and we also do it across the country. The same foundation, the same approach we have taken with Love Modesto applies to Love Our Cities as well. We champion what our partner cities are doing. We help to train them and give them support. We work to connect them with one another so that we can all learn, we can all get better at loving our cities.

Being willing to champion others has had another long term and frankly unexpected benefit for us. Because we have been consistently willing to help and to promote others, we have met a lot of people we probably wouldn't have otherwise. We have made connections and learned more about how we can really help our city. Even more, we have become the go to for getting things done in the community. People and organizations know and trust us, they know we have made contacts all over and they send people to us. We have become a hub, a neutral convener in and for our community.

The Power of a Neutral Convener

And what, you may ask, is a neutral convener? It doesn't exactly slide off the tongue, we know, but it is exactly what we are. Love Modesto started to really grow once we moved out of a single church building. That simple move was a signal that others could be a part of what we were doing, that this was not a territorial thing, not an "us" thing. It was neutral. That neutrality is a really, really big deal. Early on it meant that we were able to bring different churches together in ways that normally didn't happen. Being neutral also meant that government agencies suddenly felt free to connect in ways that just wouldn't have worked if we were at a specific church or even had that church's name.

The importance of neutrality probably can't be understated, but just as important is being a "convener". We are the group that gets things done. We put on a huge event in the community and everyone knows it. We have become really good at organizing volunteers and getting them engaged in projects. We are Airbnb, right? But it's bigger than just an individual project and volunteers.

Earlier we mentioned "sectors" in our community. Business and government, nonprofits, churches, schools and the wider community. Many times these sectors don't really talk to one another, even when an individual likely has roles in several of them. Often these sectors are highly territorial and suspicious of one another. And even when they do make connections those connections are limited. They look something like this:

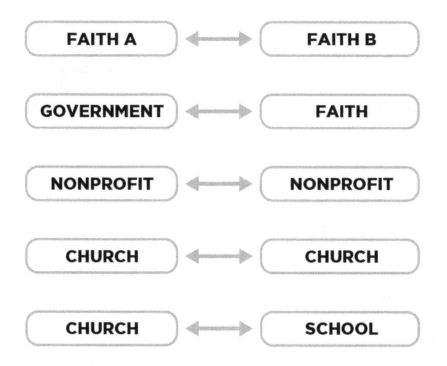

The connections may be real, they may be working, but they only work in two directions. But when a neutral convener comes into the equation, the whole picture changes:

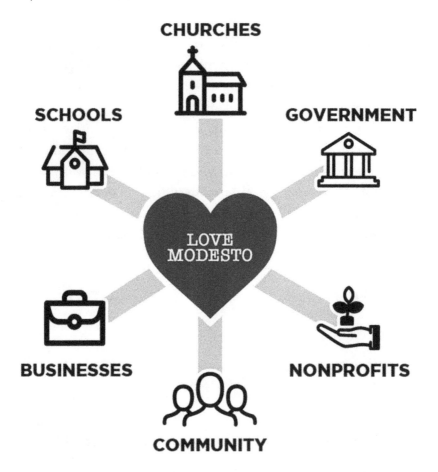

Love Modesto functions as the hub. This is the uniqueness of what we do. We are the neutral center that allows all of the sectors in a given city to come together. We facilitate connections in a way that is simply not possible otherwise. As a neutral party that is helping promote projects that matter to the various sectors in the community, we become the link that allows them to play together.

When you are humble and build relationships, you've earned the right to sit at the table and be a part of the larger picture, and the people in the various sectors, in the organizations within these sectors, see the value of partnering with you. When we get out of our silos, we realize that other sectors (government, nonprofits, etc.) are having the same conversations over the same issues, usually at a much higher level than just us, and when we interact, there are more holistic solutions that have longer lasting effects.

As I mentioned in a previous chapter, early on I had a couple of pastors ask if we had to meet at Big Valley. They were concerned because it wasn't a neutral location. The identification of Love Modesto with a specific church was hurting our ability to cross lines. Those pastors, those churches shared our common vision of loving our town, but there was a higher barrier to entry because of the direct connection to Big Valley. It wasn't an insurmountable barrier, but it was there. We've seen similar things in other cities. In one city a church did the wrap up video for the event. Their logo went at the end. It wouldn't have been a big deal, except that theirs was the *only* logo included. Other churches and businesses felt slighted and a video meant to celebrate what had occurred ended up causing disunity.

We've learned from those experiences. In order to be a neutral convener, you really have to be neutral. That means planning meetings need to occur at a neutral site or they need to rotate. It means that the logos of churches and nonprofits who partner and support our events go in the background not up front. It means paying attention to things that may not seem like a big deal to you, but which help maintain neutrality so that everyone feels that they have an equal seat at the table.

Being the neutral convener in town is more providing a networking opportunity or a chance to interact across lines. We have visibility throughout the community that matters no matter whether you are a business or a nonprofit, a school or a foster agency. That matters. It motivates and gets attention. It is bigger than any one group or cause. Our branding and our event drive the engine of community engagement. We have seen this happen in Modesto and around the country. Take Love Modesto as an example:

When the county wanted to get the faith community connected with what was going on with their Focus on Prevention program, they called us.

When COVID hit and the community needed a way to organize a hotline for people to receive food, coordinate volunteers to pick up and deliver that food from local pantries, they called us. They knew we had the ear of all the community and could rally the troops quickly.

United Way decided to stop its volunteer portal and partner with Love Modesto instead because they knew we had the momentum as the volunteer hub in the community.

Building a Brand that Unites

Brands are everywhere. The best brands connect to their customers instantly, without thought. A single word evokes more than a thought or image, but a feeling. Apple, Starbucks, the NFL. All brands that instantly connect, that instantly and powerfully convey meaning. People think of Apple and immediately images of style and cool, of artistry come to mind. Brands convey identity and they can unite or divide us easily. Coke vs Pepsi; the Yankees vs everyone; Democrats vs Republicans. It doesn't really matter which side of any of those you are on, they unite some people and divide others. Any one of the sectors, and any one of the groups within those sectors can and often does the same. But if we are going to really help our communities, if we really want to love our cities, we have to unify people. We have to get Coke and Pepsi drinkers to work together, we have to overlook the fact that some of you are actually Yankee fans (I'm kidding!), and yes, we have to work across political lines in order to make things happen.

The Love Modesto brand had five immediate things going for it. Five things that made it a unifying force in our city. Five things that really helped us to establish our identity as a neutral convener. Simplicity. Commonality. Identity. Power. Repeatability.

L♥ve Modesto

Simplicity

Love Modesto. It's not really that hard to figure out. There's no code. No explanation. Two words. A simple font. A heart for the "o" in Love. Black. White. Red. Simple.

Simplicity matters in branding because you have to capture people's attention immediately. If you want to unite people you have to get their attention. Simple gets the ball rolling.

Commonality

Our branding helps us to unite people because it gets to the heart of what we have in common. It doesn't divide. We keep saying it—people love where they are from. Or they want to. Keeping that common place, common idea and ideal at the center of our brand is important. It keeps us at the center, the hub. It doesn't identify us with a specific faith or church, with a government program or a cause. It allows us to function as the neutral convener, to cross lines and become the facilitator to help our cities.

Identity

Love is our why. Our branding reflects that. That simple, common element breaks down barriers. It speaks to who we are and what we are about. Bottom line, it conveys our heart in a single word. Communicating that heart to our community and to the people we partner with is crucial. It's also an everyday reminder to us that this is not about programs or events, it's not about territory or causes. It's about people. It's about loving our city.

Power

There is something inherently powerful in our branding. People respond to it instinctively. It genuinely connects all kinds of people. People who would probably not cross paths otherwise. It unites people in common cause for the betterment of their city. It allows people with different causes and different outlooks to come together. That is truly powerful.

Repeatable

The true test of brand power is whether or not it works in different situations, in different places with different kinds of people. Our branding works in California and in North Carolina, in Connecticut and Colorado. It is repeatable.

This branding stuff probably sounds like a commercial. It's not intended to. We are not claiming that we are completely original here or somehow smarter than everyone else. Far from it. But the truth is, our branding has helped us to be a neutral convener in the cities we work with. It has helped us to raise our profile and function as a hub that can bring people to the table and drive projects forward. We have become a brand that unites both where we live and across the country. That has been exciting for us because we have been able to help more people. The brand has helped us to identify and help a lot of great organizations in the community that are dying for help and partnership. We are helping them to further their efforts.

When others are successful in our city, we're successful. As THE neutral convener, we are able to let everyone know about what is going on, to help shine light on what is happening in our communities. We believe that we're a better community when we are behind each other, and as the neutral convener in town, we're positioned best to do it because we have a volunteer day that brings everyone together.

City-Wide Volunteer Day

By this point a lot of you are probably thinking "this is all well and good, I get it, I'm on board, but tell me what you actually do. I mean, you started this whole thing off by telling us about what happened at the last volunteer day in Modesto. Tell us about that already."

Done.

The why and the how is really important. All of the foundations and underpinnings of what we do are crucial, even the branding which everyone loves and wants to be a part of doesn't really matter if it's not connected to something that actually works. That's where it all has to come together. All of the stuff we have talked about for the last two chapters—compassion and humility, collaboration—it's the stuff behind the walls when you flip a house. It's the electrical and the plumbing, the insulation and the HVAC system. It is all needed, but it doesn't sell the house. Finishes sell the house. The city-wide volunteer day is a really practical, tangible event. It serves as both a catalyst for change and momentum builder for a movement of community engagement.

There are a lot of details that go into pulling off a city-wide volunteer day. We will talk about the nuts and bolts of it all in chapter 8, but first we need to talk about what the event does.

Catalyst for Change

The great recession was the catalyst for Love Modesto. The crisis meant that needs were no longer hidden. We had to do something. Our first events were a response to that need. In turn, Love Modesto became a catalyst for others in our community and surrounding communities (which were hit just as hard as we were) to step in and do something. As people saw what we were doing, as we invited them to be a part of what we were doing, the event became a natural catalyst.

In chemistry, the catalyst is the agent that speeds up a chemical reaction. Basically, the catalyst is necessary to increase the output of the reaction. You can get things done without it, but it is going to take longer, be less efficient and just not produce as much of the desired result. That's the way the city-wide volunteer event works.

When the economy tanked in Modesto in 2007 everyone realized that something had to change. It simply wasn't possible for the government to handle all of the needs. It wasn't possible for churches to do everything. It wasn't possible for our local nonprofits to handle the increase in needs in the community. We didn't realize it at the time, but our church-wide volunteer day which became a city-wide volunteer day, was the catalyst for change that our city needed.

Community service projects did get done before Love Modesto existed. Cleaning up the parks, removing graffiti, Habitat for Humanity houses—if I thought long enough, I could probably think of a hundred different projects. But all of those projects, all of those causes lived in relative obscurity: individual churches or organizations would do service projects, but just like First Saturdays, they often didn't get a lot of notice or participation.

Our one-day event became a catalyst for change because it had a low barrier to entry for the average person. We had unifying branding from the very beginning which increased visibility in our church. Once we went out to the community and got better at promoting, combined with the relationships we were building, it became pretty clear to lots of people that this event was doing something that previous efforts had not been able to achieve. We were changing the way that things were getting done in our town. The fact that we have been able to repeat this process in city after city across California and the country is a pretty good indicator that it wasn't a fluke. It wasn't just the fact of the recession or where we were that made this work. The one-day event, properly executed, was really up to something. It changed the dynamic of what was going on. Because we were bringing all of these different sectors and groups together in a way that no one had before, we were increasing the efficiency of the interaction, just like a catalyst in a chemistry experiment. But it didn't stop there.

Momentum Builder

Not only did the city-wide volunteer day change the way people thought about getting our community engaged, it also became a momentum builder. As we outlined in the earlier chapters, we started out with multiple events every year. It took us a while, but eventually we realized that this was a mistake. We were sucking up too much energy and not putting enough back into the system. All of the time, energy and effort that it took to put on a really good event was overwhelming both to the people responsible for making it happen and for the people who volunteered. Sure, we got participation in the second and third events, but it always went down as the year progressed.

By moving to once a year, the city-wide volunteer day functions better. We optimized the power input and the output got better. We kept it in the spring when new life was popping, and people wanted to be out and active. People could also see the visible signs of things needing to be done outside because we had just come through winter—a spring clean-up was in order. (Yes, all you Northerners and Midwesterners we know, you have real winter, and we don't here in California. The point still stands.) The signs around the community and the big rally downtown made the volunteer day an event. Everyone wanted to be a part of it.

Every year since we moved to our current model in Modesto, we have seen increased numbers of volunteers. We have been able to increase the number of projects and we have been able to showcase what different organizations do. Here's where the momentum is really compounded—not only do more people want to be a part of what's going on, but more people also end up continuing to be a part of the organizations whose projects they volunteer for in the one-day event. We see it over and over. If people have a good experience with the project they work on, a lot will stick with that project the next year. As we mentioned earlier, if the project leader is doing a good job, chances are that the volunteer will do more than just the one-day project.

To use another analogy, the one-day city-wide volunteer day acts as a flywheel. In your car, the flywheel is the part that transfers energy from the engine to the transmission. It stores energy, smooths it out and then transfers it so that the transmission can drive the wheels. If you didn't have a flywheel, you would have a very jerky ride: a power surge then nothing, power surge then nothing. The flywheel absorbs the energy from the engine, stores it, then transfers it in a smooth, circular motion. The same principle applies for the one-day event and the ongoing needs of an organization or cause. When the one-day event is done well, it provides power for a project or organization. When the leader of that project does a good job of connecting with those volunteers, that momentum is carried on throughout the year, smoothing out the ride. But it gets even better. In a car the flywheel is relatively small. It has to be for obvious reasons—a car is only so big, extra weight is a problem and so on. Because we aren't talking about cars or really about physics at all, the one-day event is also able to get bigger, to store and release more energy. That means if we do all the other stuff right, if we keep our "why" on track by humbly caring for people, if we pay attention to our "how" by developing and maintaining trusting relationships, then the "what" of the one-day event grows organically. The flywheel gets bigger and bigger as more people get involved.

We suppose there are limits to how big the flywheel can get, but we haven't found them yet. The more we do this, the better we get at it, the more we can make the event work harder. Bringing all of this together the way we do is what has made Love Modesto and Love Our Cities successful for over a decade. That's what we are going to explore in the next section.

City Spotlight:
Costa Mesa, California

Year Joined: 2018
City Leader: Ian Stevenson

Tell us a bit about your city:
Costa Mesa is a city of 115,000 that sits on a hill just inland of Newport Beach and south of Huntington Beach in the midst of the 3.3 million people and 34 cities that make up the urban sprawl that is Orange County, CA. Our history dates back to the 1880's when settlers started living in the area. A sleepy farming community in the early 1900's, the first school, church, fire station and railway led to a growing community. The establishment of a United States Air Corp Replacement Training Base in the 1940's added to its growth and in 1953 Costa Mesa was incorporated, becoming its own city. In the late 1960s the city evolved and grew again with the development of the 405 freeway and the South Coast Plaza, one of the premier destination shopping sites of the west coast, in the north end. Costa Mesa is a primarily working-class Hispanic and Caucasian community with a variety of neighborhoods and housing styles.

Costa Mesa is becoming known as a city of the Arts, with the development of the Orange County Performing Arts Center which hosts many nationally acclaimed performances. We are home of the Orange County Fairgrounds which hosts millions of visitors each year as well as being the current home of the LA Chargers.

What do you love about Costa Mesa, and what are some of the unique challenges you face?
Costa Mesa is a fun place to be with lots to do: close to the beach, the premier shopping location on the west coast, the Segerstrom Performing Arts Center, the Orange County Fairgrounds and

more. We are known for incredible restaurants and being an eclectic community. While we are 50% Caucasian and 40 % Hispanic, like most of Orange County, our diversity continues to grow.

The housing crisis in California means homelessness is our greatest practical challenge. There is a huge need for affordable housing in our city and bridging the divide between the working class and the higher middle-class families is a significant need. Costa Mesa is also home to one of the largest recovery communities per capita in the country. More than half of the elementary schools in our city are title one schools where a majority of the students are on free and reduced lunch and there are challenges with test scores on literacy and math.

How did you hear about Love Our Cities and how has Love Our Cities helped you?

We heard about Love Our Cities through our friend Jay Williams in Fullerton who leads OC United. Love Our Cities' platform for establishing a city-wide volunteer day has been a huge help. The website template and software for project and volunteer sign up has been turnkey and easy to implement with what we were already doing and has helped us involve more and more of our community in caring for the city. The calls to learn from other cities and coaching on developing sponsors and engaging more non-profits, churches, businesses and the city have been extremely helpful, stimulating our growth. Visiting the event in Modesto gave our team a bigger vision for what could be, and their team has been helpful any time we have questions or have asked for feedback on various ideas.

Tell us about your city-wide volunteer day and other efforts you have undertaken:

Our organization, Trellis, had already been working on an ongoing basis in the city for several year facilitating collaboration in the city around prayer, neighboring, education and homelessness. As a result, we already had buy-in and a good reputation in the city. We did our first Love Costa Mesa Day in May of 2018 with the goal of making this a new, annual activity that our neighboring initiative was going to take ownership for running in the city. With just over 300 volunteers doing 26 projects it was a great start. Right from the beginning we involved 15 churches, city hall, several businesses and multiple non-profits. In 2019, we had over 1,000 volunteers participate in 49 projects.

As an organization that really focuses on ongoing collaboration throughout the year, the city-wide volunteer day allowed us to have numerous projects that impacted each of our four main initiatives, involve even more churches, nonprofits and businesses. City hall was ecstatic, and Love Costa Mesa Day is now some of our city council members favorite day! Running this event for the city has developed good will with leaders, neighbors, churches and brought more and more awareness in our community of ongoing ways people can make a difference in our city.

What others are saying:

"Love Costa Mesa Day is one of my favorite days of the year! It's an opportunity to come together with friends and neighbors to do work that improves our community. Thank you to Trellis for their hard work to make this happen every year. "

—Andrea Marr, Costa Mesa City Council Member

"When I decided to get involved in Love Costa Mesa Day, it opened my heart to others. Once I saw the needs of others, my relationships with my neighbors slowly grew. I found it wasn't only about the task but earning another's cooperation, trust and appreciation. I saw it bring others together and break down division. I've also seen many others in my city want to reach out. There's awesome power in this—as this grows, I've seen friendships and partnerships grow. They can be unified as a team, and I enjoy being a part of it. People in need get to see that they're not alone. I've found a new purpose, one that's still growing. I would've never experienced any of this if I hadn't jumped in to help."

—Ralph Hulett, Costa Mesa Resident

"Love Costa Mesa has brought unity to a community, where people from all walks of life, businesses, and other organizations come to together to serve and make our city better...together."

—Ben Glassman, Community Member

"I haven't missed a LCM Day yet! I don't intend to in the future. The value of this day is that the opportunity to serve just for a one and done event is that I see it changes hearts, minds and attitudes. I know on this day I am part of a bigger plan! This is where divine intervention occurs. Young, old, families, students, church folks and city workers. There are no isms, schisms just prisms of God's love that leaves a lasting mark on everyone who participates. I consider it an honor to be asked to serve. I know others do as well."

—Charlene M. Ashendorf, long time Costa Mesa Resident

Part 3:

The Secret Sauce

Here's the part where we start getting really practical. To this point we have told you our story, we have given you glimpses of what Love Modesto and Love Our Cities have done for over a decade. We have given you the foundational principles for why, how, and what we do. It's all necessary stuff, but I am guessing that if you are at all like us, especially if you are like Jeff, you want to get to the practical stuff. How do you make this happen? This is the part where you start putting things together, where you start thinking about your city and what could happen there.

Lots of restaurants make lots of great food, but, from fast food joints to your local favorite, there's just something about the secret sauce that makes that one place unique. It doesn't matter if it's Chinese or Mexican or even grandma's red sauce, (we're from California so when it comes to burgers you know we're partial to In 'N Out), the secret sauce just can't be duplicated, and it keeps you coming back.

There are lots of organizations that do lots of great things just like there are lots of similar restaurants. We mentioned the secret sauce in the last chapter. Here's where you get a peek at our recipe, the thing that we do to help you maximize your impact in your city, the thing that has over 100 cities partnering with us right now. What we've found is pretty simple: the way to get things moving is to start with a City-Wide Volunteer Day.

You love your city. You want to help it to be better. The City-Wide Volunteer Day is the way to focus that energy, to build a flywheel that will begin that process. In this section we will explore the crucial mindset you need, the nuts and bolts of a volunteer day, and how to build off of the momentum your city-wide volunteer day will bring.

Think of it this way, we have spent over 12 years developing what we do. We have made the mistakes, had breakthroughs, created plans and systems. We have refined and improved the sauce. We have worked with over 100 different cities and over 225,000 volunteers to bring over 1,000,000 volunteer hours totaling over $28.5 million worth of service. People keep coming back for the secret sauce. This section starts the process of distilling all of that information so that you don't need a decade to get the sauce ready.

Let's get cooking.

Stop Doing Things
for Your City

"There comes a point where we need to stop just pulling people out of the river. We need to go upstream and find out why they're falling in."

— Desmond Tutu

It seemed like a good plan. The neighborhood had lots of needs. It was an eyesore. The alleys, vacant lots, and streets were overgrown and full of trash. We saw the need and we were going to help, to fix it. This was pre-Love Modesto. We organized, we actually got a lot of people to come out and we descended on the neighborhood.

We had garbage bins filled to the brim. We cleaned up a *lot* of stuff. We took before and after photos, there's probably video somewhere. Some people came outside wondering what was going on. Not everyone was happy: "Hey why are you taking that? That's my stuff!"

We couldn't understand why "these people" didn't appreciate what we were doing, why they didn't welcome us. I drove through that neighborhood a week later. One week. It looked the same as it had before we had been there. It was like we had never been there. All that work. All that time and effort. All those good intentions. Nothing to show for it.

What went wrong?

We screwed up. Plain and simple. We got ahead of ourselves. The people of that neighborhood felt invaded. Our hearts were in the right place. We saw a need and wanted to fix it. We had some compassion. We put it into action. But we didn't think it through. We weren't exactly arrogant about it, but we were certainly ignorant. We didn't put ourselves in the shoes of the people who lived in that neighborhood. Honestly, we were looking at a service project not at people. Here's a problem that we can fix. Here's something we can do for the neighborhood.

There was a problem baked into the thinking. It wasn't intentional. There was no ill will. I truly believe we had the best of intentions and a good heart. But we had blind spots and didn't know it. We needed a better MAP: Mindset, Approach, Payoff.

Mindset: With not For

Chances are you have been there too. Some service project, some program or idea that fell flat on its face. In fact, you might have had the opposite effect. Perhaps, like us, you didn't think about the project from the point of view of the neighborhood. It's not the end of the road, but you do have to recognize the problem.

It's a problem of mindset: an "us and them" mentality. You may not even realize you have it. Honestly, the people you want to help might have it too. But it's a problem that must be overcome. It's a problem that can be overcome. The simplest way to start down this path is to start by changing one simple preposition.

Stop doing things *for* that neighborhood.
Stop doing things *for* the community.
Stop doing things *for* the city.

Start doing things *with* that neighborhood.
Start doing things *with* the community.
Start doing things *with* the city.

With not for.

When we change this simple preposition, our mindset shifts. It starts us down a path that is almost inevitable. It's contagious. *With* creates partnership. It creates ownership in the best sense of the term.

For has a tendency to create ownership in the worst sense of the word. The people doing the project have a tendency to believe that it is *their* project. This was our idea. We have the means, the know-how, and the intelligence or education to see and fix the problem that you clearly do not. *For* has a tendency to get a savior complex. *For* often leads to us doing what we do simply so that we can feel good about ourselves. Look at how enlightened we are. How much we care. Us and them.

I want to be careful at this point. A lot of people think about doing things *for* others with really good intentions. It's all they have ever known or been taught. There is a good heart underneath it that doesn't even see the condescension going on. Honestly, that's where the team who cleaned up that neighborhood were. It's where I was. There's a difference between not knowing or just not thinking through something, and arrogance. One attitude you can fix, and the other one maybe not.

When you have a *for* mentality you see need and projects that need to be done. If you are sharp, you may even be seeing the real needs and have come up with useful projects and causes. So you start moving, you start organizing and getting your hands dirty. Usually, the problem with a *for* mindset is a problem of direction not intention. We've seen a lot of good intentions go awry. A couple of examples spring to mind.

There was the backpack drive for underprivileged kids. Great idea. Terrible execution. Several churches dropped off backpacks. Some schools ended up sending multiple backpacks home with a single kid because there were more backpacks than kids. What was supposed to be a good thing ended up being wasteful and a headache for school administrators. The problem: no one coordinated with the schools.

In another city there's a line of 200 people outside of The Salvation Army for dinner at one of their facilities. A church rolls up alongside in a bunch of vans, opens the doors and starts to feed people. Half the people in line eat and leave. 100 meals go to waste inside. The desire to help wasn't bad. At the very least the planning was terrible. It's really tempting to think that they just didn't care about the implications—it wasn't like they went to a park or something, they went right outside the doors of the place that everyone knows feeds people in need.

In a pretty major city in California the city government asked the churches in the area to stop feeding the homeless. Again, it wasn't the heart to help that was the problem. It was the lack of coordination and in fact the duplication of programs already in place to help.

This is where all the lessons from Part 2 come into focus. For the record, we are also not saying that the city or county has all the answers. We aren't saying that you don't have good ideas or motives. We are saying that when you have a *for* mentality you will never know because you didn't take the time to get the information you needed. When you adopt a *with* mentality that changes.

I can hear the objections:

"You have never been to my town."

"The local government is corrupt."

"The people in charge are totally incompetent."

"The churches don't care about anyone outside their walls."

"There isn't anyone besides the government to go to."

Maybe you're right. Maybe you just think you are right. Here's the thing. In city after city across the country, we have always found someone stepping up. *Always.* We have worked with over one hundred cities and we have never seen a situation where there wasn't someone. Maybe the government really is a mess. I bet the local non-profits or churches are stepping in. If you happen to find that one situation where no one actually exists, well, maybe you are the person who has to fill that void.

Side note: I know that it is popular to blame "the government" for lots of the ills in society. I get it. But two things stick out to me that I don't think we pay enough attention to when we complain. First, in the United States, we are the government. We can participate and do something about the situation we are in, so if the government is corrupt, well, that's on us. We have to fix it. Second, and more importantly, most of the corruption in government happens at the elected official level. The vast majority of interactions that we have, that you will have when you start something in your city, are rank and file employees, the ones who usually work where they do because they actually care about that work. They actually do care about the affordable housing problem or providing decent, safe parks or helping kids with nowhere to go. They're not an elected official with an agenda, and most likely they are there because they want to help. Chances are they see the problems just like you do.

When we started Love Modesto, we made a point of working not to repeat our past. We have tried very hard to build the mindset of "with not for" into everything we do. We train our partner cities this way. We don't always get it right, but we are always trying to get better. A *with* mentality says let's talk to these neighborhoods first. Let's talk to homeowners first. Let's talk to our city first. Let's talk to our schools first. Let's have this posture of learning more about what they're doing, and also saying, "Hey, we think we are seeing a need here. We are planning to do something to help, would you want to join? We would love your help with this."

Approach: Get the lay of the land

I have thought a lot about what I would do differently today if we were going to do a project in that neighborhood. The first person I would call is Armando Nunez. He's a key person on staff at Orville Wright Elementary School and leads the Airport District Collaborative. It wasn't around back when we did our project. We didn't help establish it. It was just concerned people in the neighborhood who decided that they needed to meet and to address issues of their neighborhood. They meet once a month. They talk about community issues. They get involved in making things better for that neighborhood.

But what if there isn't a collaborative? What could we have done better back then when Armando wasn't the guy? Start by asking the right questions. *Who are the players* in that neighborhood, in your city? Who's in the know? Who are the people doing things, the natural built-in community leaders already there? Start with the principal of the neighborhood school. The pastors of the churches in the area. Chances are there are local non-profits, businesses who care about their neighborhood, clubs and civic groups like the Rotary or the PTA. Talk to the local city councilman. If the town is smaller, then talk to the mayor's office. *Find the players.* Start with the people you know and move out from there. Everyone knows someone. Even if you don't know the right someone, someone else does. It takes a bit of detective work, but you can find them. Get out of your silo.

Once you have found the players, actually as you are looking for the right players, your number one goal is simple: listen. Not fix the problem, not present a giant vision or a plan to solve all of the problems. Listen. Remember the mindset— "with not for". Make it a part of who you are. With means you don't have all the answers and you know that you don't have all the answers.

As a leader, you have no doubt thought about the problem a lot. Chances are you have 14 different ideas and ways to help. Your natural inclination is going to be "hey, we can fix this". Bite your tongue. I know it's hard. I have been there. I am the king of charge in and get it done. I am not saying that you have no good ideas or that you shouldn't offer any solutions. I am saying not yet. Be patient. Learn the lay of the land. Find out what the local players know.

I guarantee you will learn something you didn't know. There will be some detail you overlooked, some organization who is already doing something and you had no idea. The more you learn the better the solutions will end up being. When people believe they are actually being heard the floodgates will open. When you listen, adopting a posture of humility that says I want to know you and your situation, trust builds. When you listen to the needs of a neighborhood or a group of people you may find that the issue that you thought needed to be addressed isn't the actual need at all. Or you may have been right about the need and by finding the right people, by listening to the neighborhood and the local leaders, you have earned the right to sit at the table, to ask questions. And I really mean ask. We've all been in class with that one guy, you know the one: he asks lots of questions, but he's never once asked a question that he didn't have an answer for. Don't be that guy. Remember Marvin's mantra from chapter 5: "Show up, shut up, and don't speak until you are asked."

Ask about the needs of the community. Ask the local businesses what they see as the problem. Ask the neighbors what the biggest issues are. Ask the city government what resources they can bring to bear. Ask how you can help, how you can be a partner. Learn what matters to people. If you are crossing cultural boundaries, make sure you are sensitive to them and that you are trying, as much as you can, to put yourself in their shoes and understand things from their point of view. I am not saying you are going to or have to agree with everything. I am saying that you have to respect people enough, care enough, about the people you say you want to help, to listen to what they think.

After you have listened, after you have asked your questions to make sure that you really understand, then you get to offer ideas. Idea being the key word. "Idea" doesn't mean that it is going to happen, that you are going to do something *for* someone. It is an offering, a possibility. When you offer up an idea, it means that you are relinquishing ownership. You are opening up the possibility that the idea isn't complete, that it needs to be tweaked. You are offering the people that you want to help the opportunity to come alongside. To have a share in the ownership of the idea and to make it work.

Listen, ask, then humbly offer your ideas. Not everyone will be on board Some will. Start there.

Payoff: Destination in Sight

Having a "with not for" mindset, approaching the community properly by finding the players and listening then asking—all of it—sets you up for something far bigger than a successful project. It sets you up to love your city in a sustainable, broadly beneficial way. If you truly want to love your city, if you want to make it different, not just "make a difference" then this approach will get you there. You get four ingredients that come together to set you up for your first city-wide volunteer day.

First things first, you need buy-in. You need *local ownership*. If we had gone to the people in the Airport District neighborhood with a "with not for" mindset before showing up to fix the problem things probably would have been different. The fact that there is a neighborhood collaborative there today tells me people there do care about their neighborhood. They came together to do something about the problems they saw. Sure, it wasn't on our timetable, but it happened. Most people, even people who care, aren't sure where to start or if they even can. They need a leader to step up, to ask the right questions, to cast a vision for what could be the case. If we would have come in and found out the needs of the neighborhood, if we would have found the people with influence and listened to their needs, we could have probably done the exact same project, but it would have been successful because the neighborhood would have owned it. We would have partnered with them, not imposed our ideas on them. That's a big difference. The idea of doing a clean-up project becomes their idea. They get to make it theirs. That kind of ownership is the kind of ownership we want to see. It's the kind of ownership that is needed if things are going to change in your city. It requires humility on your part, and that leads to real partnership. Guess what, when you have partners you don't feel like you are unwanted—because you aren't.

Local ownership will also increase participation. If you are an outside group parachuting into a neighborhood or community to fix things for them, I guarantee participation from that community will be low. Maybe even nonexistent. They don't know who you are, they don't know if they should trust you, and they probably didn't even know that you are coming until you showed up. But if you worked with the community to under-stand what was needed, to plan what the event was going to look like and what was going to get accomplished? If that neighborhood owns the idea? You will definitely get more participation from them.

When I was trying to make First Saturdays happen it pretty much didn't work. It was my idea. I owned it, no one else really did. When we started Love Modesto, we laid the groundwork first. Our church Leader-ship was on the same page. We put together a vision and let the people of the church know about it. We involved others in what was going to happen. They owned it. Because of all of those things our very first event blew me out of the water. Over ten times the amount of people I was hoping for and over 100 times the amount of people who were regularly coming out for First Saturdays showed up. Yes, it took a lot of work to get us to that point—six months of planning and preparation, but it all paid off. It paid off bigtime. When people participate in something that they feel ownership in, momentum starts. Momentum leads to the third key ingredient of your payoff: *sustainability.*

One of the biggest things that has to be overcome in both physics and in community engagement is inertia. In physics, inertia is basically the property of matter that says unless you apply force of some kind to an object it will keep doing what it is doing. If it isn't moving, well, it's pretty much going to stay there. If it's moving, it will keep moving. The same thing applies in community engagement.

Chances are the problems of a neighborhood or a city are what they are because there isn't an adequate force to overcome them. Maybe, like Modesto in 2008, they are getting worse because of the outside force of the recession. We needed something to change. It took something new and different, a force that had not been applied before, to help overcome not just inertia, but the momentum of a city headed in the wrong direc-tion.

Back to the airport neighborhood. If we had done what we should have done, what we started doing with Love Modesto, we could have helped to counter the inertia of a neighborhood in crisis. We have seen this over and over again in Modesto and around the country. The more listening and asking we did, the more we started to do stuff *with* the neighborhood, local ownership went up, participation went up, and that meant sustainability went up. When the people in the neighborhood own the idea, when they are working to clean it up, there's not going to be as much garbage the following week, because it's theirs. They helped clean it up, so they don't want to see it go back to what it was before. Sustainability is built right in.

This is where the city-wide volunteer day really shines. The "with not for" mindset is sort of the fuel. The big one-day event takes all of that positive energy and stores it, transfers it just like a flywheel and keeps the energy flowing back into the community at a regular rate. You have to pay attention of course, you have to put the effort in to create the local partnerships and to get participation, you have to make sure that you are doing your part by helping create the infrastructure and running a successful event, but if you do then sustainability is part of the package. You have successfully overcome inertia. And when that happens people notice. When people notice, the fourth ingredient of the payoff comes into play: *recognition.*

Here's the thing about doing things for your community. No one cares. No one notices. Maybe the lady whose yard you cleaned up does. Maybe people notice the local park looks a bit neater. Probably they think the grounds crew finally got around to cleaning things up and they don't pay it much mind. In three weeks it will be back to where it was.

Even with Love Modesto, as successful as it was in the very first event, we were one church. We had stumbled on the idea of "with not for" when it came to getting people in our congregation involved, but we hadn't yet taken the next step. We sort of applied it outside of the church, but not consistently. We didn't really understand at the time just how significant it was.

Once we started thinking this way holistically, applying the approach of listening to the various players in the community, everything changed. We were no longer doing an event for the community; we were providing an opportunity for the entire community to come together and work with one another. We were truly becoming the neutral convener. And people noticed.

The media showed up. They started talking about what we were doing. The nonprofits in town started to come to us with projects they wanted to be a part of the next city-wide volunteer day. We were able to work more closely with the schools and with the local government because they knew who we were, and they knew that we were going to work *with* them. When you gain recognition like that the flywheel can (and does) get bigger.

Today Love Modesto is one of the key players at the table for community engagement. We are the neutral convener in the city and everyone—government, nonprofits, businesses, local churches, the media—everyone knows it. That's not an accident. We wanted to make things better in the city. We knew that we could not do it alone. We realized that by adopting a mindset that was fundamentally different we could better achieve that purpose. At the end of the day, it is really all about the people not the projects. The projects themselves, as important as they are, are simply the means to an end. We love our city. We want it to be better. That means helping people. The city-wide volunteer day has become our single best means of generating momentum, of applying enough force to the situation to overcome inertia and set things off in a better direction.

It's not a small task. Crafting a truly successful city-wide volunteer day takes effort. It takes planning and know how. It takes a good team. But like we said, we can help with that—it's our secret sauce. Let's get into the nuts and bolts.

City Spotlight:
Hartford, Connecticut

Year Joined: 2017
City Leader: Lauren Roy

Tell us a bit about your city:
The insurance capital of the world, Hartford is also Connecticut's capital city and one of the oldest cities in the country—it was established in 1635! Hartford has seen lots of history: it is home to the oldest continuously operating newspaper in the US (The Hartford Courant), the revolver (Colt), gas pump counter, gold fillings, first American dictionary and air-cooled airplane engines among other things. Hartford was founded by Puritan leader Thomas Hooker who settled on the banks of the Connecticut River. He had a vision of a government run by the people and his influence has left Connecticut with the notable and influential title of "Constitution state". Even before the English established Hartford, there was a Dutch trading post nearby and Native American tribes including the Saukiog, Poduck and Tunxis.

Hartford is a city composed of many distinct neighborhoods that vary by race, income, employment and other factors. Many people might be surprised to learn that over 45% of Hartford is Hispanic or Latino and 36% African American. There are seventeen neighborhoods that make up the city and each one brings a uniqueness of its own! Many people including those working in the insurance industry commute into the city leaving the downtown area rather empty on weekends and after 5pm. Outside of downtown many neighborhoods, organizations and churches are active beyond the 9-5 weekday hours.

What do you love about Hartford, and what are some of the unique challenges you face?

A city rich in the arts, filled with change agents passionate about justice, committed to supporting and loving their neighbors well; I am proud to be part of the city of Hartford. I love the connectedness of organizations and people. It is really amazing to see the overlap of people, churches and organizations working together to create a stronger impact. Just a few examples: the Urban Alliance network pairs ministries and churches for service, the Hartford Project does an incredible job as well and so does the Center for Leadership and Justice which actively organizes to make the community better and is known for their work around slumlords and interfaith organizing. Billings Forge is an organization that uses food as a way for community empowerment and job training. We have significant issues that are tough and will require continued hard work and collaboration. By some estimates over 20% of Hartford's population were born outside of the US. Poverty is a big issue for our city—the poverty rate has been over 30% in recent years. The Church is active in Hartford, with many individual churches actively serving the community through sending volunteers or leading basic needs programs and many other programs.

I love that Hartford seems to understand that greater impact, whether meeting a basic need or fighting for housing equity, is found in our collective voice and effort. I love that Hartford is the Capital city. It holds a unique weight in our state and region. The church in Hartford has the potential for statewide impact. I can already see this in the connection with the surrounding suburbs, which are connected through the commuter population. Hartford has the opportunity for regional impact—from surrounding towns to the state as a whole. Its location sets Hartford up to be a change agent in the state as a whole, and over the past year we have seen it as a place of influence through protests, especially in regard to racism. This unique attribute sets it apart as a leader in the state. I love this unique quality of Hartford and it encourages me about its current impact and that in the future.

How did you hear about Love Our Cities and how has Love Our Cities helped you?

We first connected with Love our Cities about two years ago when we were looking to do a collaborative day of service with several local organizations and churches. We were looking for an online platform that would provide a space for people to see the variety of service opportunities and sign-up to be a part of the day also. Love Our Cities provided just that! We loved how the platform created a user-friendly space for people to see the selection of service day projects and choose where they wished to serve.

Love Our Cities also created the space for other city leaders and organizers to connect on a regular basis. These forums provide an ongoing opportunity to learn from others and glean best practices surrounding a variety of topics from those who had planned these types of serving days prior. It has been an asset for our team to be among these leaders to continue to grow in our own development and learning too.

Tell us about your city-wide volunteer day and other efforts you have undertaken:

Love Our Cities has helped us to build stronger connections with organizations, individuals, and churches in our city. Relationships were formed during the planning stages for the volunteer day and because of that on-going partnerships have been formed and strengthened.

What others are saying:

"Your donations, help delivering supplies, and direct participation have been an absolute blessing this year. Thanks to partners like you we've served with 150+ volunteers, from 15 churches to bless over 1,500 people with care packages, essential supplies, Bibles, and more!" – The Hartford Project

"A statement on the impact that city-wide serving makes!"

"I love helping our community and making a difference. Thank you so much for organizing such a great event. We love it!"

Nuts and Bolts

Never walk away from someone who deserves help; your hand is
God's hand for that person.

— Proverbs 3:27 The Message

What's the Big Idea?

It's the middle of March. Sally is visiting Modesto for the first time. Everywhere she turns there's a Love Modesto sign: in yards, on billboards, big 4 foot by 8-foot signs in vacant lots and in the front of businesses. The bank has an "I Love Modesto" decal on the door. Everywhere she looks she sees a sign. Finally, when she stops in at Starbucks for a latte, she asks the barista what the deal is with all the signs. The barista's face lights up and she starts to talk about what's coming in a couple of weeks.

We jokingly call the city-wide volunteer day our gateway drug to community engagement. Low barrier to entry, high energy, and by now everyone wants to get in on the action. We spent a lot of time telling you our story, talking a lot about the effort that it takes to make connections in the community, about how you have to build a solid foundation of compassion and humility. This is where it all comes together.

The reality is that most people are busy. The guy in the neighborhood working a 9 to 5 and the woman running the local nonprofit. Getting people on board to help their community is not always easy. That's why everything that we have talked about so far has led to the city-wide volunteer day. This one event is the engine that drives community engagement. It makes it easy for people to participate. It doesn't demand any more commitment than a few hours on one Saturday morning and it starts with a party. What's not to love?

Making it easy for people to get on board is crucial to the success of the event and building momentum for community engagement in your city. When you do it right you get the people of your city engaged, you give the services and nonprofits in your city a boost of positive energy and momentum, you even contribute dollars to the economy because local businesses will benefit directly and indirectly from the day. You also build your place as the neutral convener in your town. Making all of that happen takes a lot of work. Here are the basics that you will need to get your city-wide volunteer day off the ground.

The Love Modesto story won't be yours—and that's a good thing for you! We had to figure everything out. From connecting and engaging to the nuts and bolts of operations, we have built a system that works. We have had a front row seat not only in Modesto, but also around the country. We have systematized what works and discarded what doesn't. We have seen cities stumble and have seen great successes along the way too. By pooling all of that knowledge we have been able to refine the process and make it much easier for you.

Before we get into the details, let me get one thing out of the way. This part is both practical and our shameless plug for partnering with Love Our Cities. We want you to be successful in creating positive community engagement in your city. We know that we aren't the only game in town. We know that you really can do this on your own, if you really want to and have the dedication—after all, that's what we did. We also believe that you shouldn't have to start from scratch because a lot of the hard work of figuring things out has already been done. This chapter is going to help you start thinking about the most significant details of getting set up. When cities partner with us, we help them from the very beginning, including "how to" guides, access to our proven branding and marketing, a best practices forum with other cities, your own website, volunteer sign up page, email marketing and even tech support. You can find the specifics at LoveOurCities.org. You don't have to partner with us to make all of this happen, and the details of this chapter could get you a long way down the path, but the costs are low, and we really think that by the end of the second year you will have more than covered the cost of the partnership (plus you get the benefit of learning from our mistakes, so you don't have to make them yourself!). OK, end of commercial, on to the nuts and bolts.

Lead Team

It all starts with a great lead team. You can make it work on your own if you have to, but it is much harder, and you will be less effective. We have found that a great lead team is a minimum of three people and ideally is formed at least nine months before the event. It's great if these three people come from three different churches in town.

Right away this raises questions: Why three? Why from churches? Why not from the mayor's office or the social one of the local nonprofits like Habitat for Humanity?

To start, we are who we are. Love Modesto started in a church. Love Our Cities was birthed out of that. This is who we are, it is fundamental to who we are, it's in our DNA. Our faith informs our entire approach. Yes, we want everyone to feel like they can be a part of what we do. Yes, we work with people from other faiths and no faith, we work with government agencies and businesses and all sorts of groups and individuals. There is no "but" here. All of this is true. AND it is because, and we really mean because our faith fuels what we do. This means that the people who sign on to partner with us sign a faith statement. It's a pretty broad one, but it is a part of both our heritage and who we are now.

There are also some practical reasons for starting with leaders from churches. The first is simple, churches start with a common starting point. All churches, at least in principle, hold the ethic of Jesus in high regard. That was at the heart of what we talked about in chapter 4. Young or old, whatever your denomination (or lack of one), no matter where you are on the political spectrum or what your specific theological bent, there is a philosophical alignment of sorts. This factor alone is crucial to getting started.

Second, the reality is that you are going to need volunteers. Churches have basically got the largest, most committed volunteer force in any given community. And we know where they are and how to get a hold of them. We really cannot stress this enough. Churches basically run on volunteers. These are people who are already involved in their communities on some level, who already believe that they should love their neighbor. They will be the start of your volunteer force. Even cities who have been quite successful at building a broad and effective city-wide volunteer day find that somewhere north of 40% of their volunteers come from churches.

Third, we need government involvement to make this work, we need the local nonprofits to be instrumental in creating a successful event. But as a rule, they are the wrong people to lead the effort. Nonprofits typically have very specific mandates—they have to in order to be effective. While you may get to the point where you have your own nonprofit entity (we will get to that later), remember, the goal is to be the neutral convener— the organization that gets everyone to the table. When you are the hub, you function differently than most nonprofits because your mandate is to bring everyone to the table to get people engaged in the community. You are, in the case of the city-wide volunteer day, the event planner organizer, cheerleader, and chief herder of cats. You need the local nonprofits to be providing different kinds of projects. Your job is to get them on the docket.

Government leaders are going to fight red tape if they try to lead the effort. Having a separate leadership, but one that is listening to both the needs and the expertise of government agencies, allows freedom of action that government leaders don't always have. When the government leads, the default thinking of many people is simply "I pay my taxes for that, so I don't really need to do anything else." That defeats the purpose. If people believe this is a government program, then they generally think that it is government funded and staffed. Neither is the case, nor should it be. Church leadership also removes the perception of partisanship on the part of government leaders. Frankly it doesn't matter which political party the leader is affiliated with; you have probably just alienated roughly 40-50%

of the population. You need to be able to diffuse political tensions, not put them on display.

So why three leaders? First, the number isn't a rule, it's a rule of thumb. Second, it is entirely practical. You need to divide up responsibilities and you need to broaden your appeal. At least to start you are not going to have your own separate organization and staff. That means your leaders are most likely going to either be volunteers or only devoting a part of their time to this project. When you include at least three different churches you automatically draw a larger volunteer base and a larger pool of connections and a broad base is important.

Set the Date

It probably seems silly but getting the date of your first city-wide volunteer date set early is crucial. Logistically speaking, everything you will be working on from this point forward stems from this date. Every project, all of the promotion, planning, everything starts from this date. As you remember from our story, we have tried all kinds of different times of the year for the city-wide volunteer day. After all of our experimentation and in basically every city we have partnered with, one time of year rises to the surface—do it in the spring.

Exactly when in the spring is a different story. Here in the central valley of California, we tend to shoot for end of April. If you are in Green Bay or upstate New York, well, you are definitely going to want to hold off a bit longer. Regardless of what part of the country you are in or exactly what month you end up doing the event, spring is still the best. There are several reasons for this.

First, there is just something about the spring that makes people want to get active. Most people have spent a considerably greater amount of time indoors than they would like for the past several months. Yes, there are places in the southwest where the opposite is true, still, the trees are starting to leaf out and bloom, the grass is starting to get green . . . life is starting over and people are tuned into that even if they don't know it.

Second, things around town tend to look a bit shabbier. Ditches and alleyways have accumulated trash over the winter. Landscaping needs cleaned up and trimmed back. Weather will have done a number on buildings. We probably all have a personal spring-cleaning urge to some degree or another. The same goes for your city.

Third, eventually, as you grow, you want people to look forward to the event. What better way to kick off summer than by bringing the community together to work together, have fun together, and generally make your city a bit better? We have found that it really does make a difference.

In order to give yourself enough time to really get all of your ducks in a row, especially for the first couple of years, you need to have the date set about 9 months in advance. That means August or September. You need to recognize that there are no perfect dates and 9 months is not absolute—we have seen events come together in 8 weeks, but the longer lead time means better organization and a fun experience for everyone. There will always be some kind of conflict or difficulty. Part of the reason you are working so far in advance is to make sure you have the best possible day you can. Check with your local community calendars—city events, school events, etc. Work around what you can but don't sweat what you cannot control.

Once you have set the date everything starts: getting your rally location nailed down, figuring out what permits and permissions you need from the city. Coordinating with the city and your partner organizations. There are a whole lot of details that really can't get worked on until the date is set. We have experienced, thought about and heard just about every conceivable issue when it comes to setting dates and getting the ball rolling and we can help you to make sure you are asking the right questions at the right time to get everything in motion at the right time and place.

Volunteer Projects

Here's the heartbeat of the day. What projects are you going to include? You have heard us talk about some of the ones that we have done. Some things are pretty universal—cleaning up parks and roadways, visiting retirement centers and helping out at local schools. Other things are going to be specific to your community. Who are the big nonprofits in town? What are the significant social needs? Are there gaps that really need to be filled? This is where all of the relationships that you have built and the knowledge you have gained about your community come into play. It's also where having a good leadership team is invaluable.

About six months before the event you need to be working on the list of projects. How many? Glad you asked. It's really pretty amazing how the math works out. Here's our basic first year formula:

City Population X 1% = Total Volunteer Spots

So, if you are a town of 15,000 people, you should plan for 150 volunteer spots. 150,000 then 1,500 spots. For the first few years, we recommend that you plan on 15 volunteers per project or for the smaller city in our example, about 10 projects. Some projects are likely to need a few more people and some less. Think of these numbers as a rule of thumb, not some immutable law that can never change or be adapted.

By year three or so you will grow the number of volunteers you have. You will probably max out at around 3-4% of your population. Modesto is around 215,000 people. In 2019 we had roughly 7500 people, or 3-4% of the population show up. The math is pretty consistent. There is one caveat I would add to this formula. If you have churches or other civic organizations who are already working on things in the community, you will probably get a higher percentage earlier. The top end numbers of 3-4% are probably not going to change all that much though.

Once you have done the math for your city and you have a target number for your volunteer projects, it's time to start lining them up. Start with a brainstorming session with your leadership team. Get lots of ideas down on paper. Not every one of them is going to pan out, that's fine. Make sure that you are bringing ideas to the table that you heard from listening to the players in the community.

As you are working on identifying your projects, you also need to be thinking about who the project leaders will be. If you are working with a local organization like Habitat for Humanity or the local foster agency, it is generally best to have that organization supply the leader if at all possible. Some of your leadership team may have specific projects that they are leading. This can work, but you need to make sure that you are able to float throughout the day of the event, offering encouragement and support where needed and being able to deal with the unexpected.

Promotion

Once you have your projects identified, it's time to let the world know what you will be doing. There are lots of ways to get the word out, but we have identified three broad categories of promotion that you need to hit well:

Web/social media

Presentations to churches, groups and events

Physical signage

Web/Social Media

For Love Modesto, everything starts with our website. If people want to learn who we are, see what we have done, sign up for a project, donate, whatever, it's all on the site. You absolutely need to have a place that is yours. Lots of organizations rely almost exclusively on Facebook and they make the mistake of letting their website languish. We can't say this strongly enough, BAD IDEA! Let's be clear, we are certainly not saying don't pay attention to Facebook. You absolutely do need to be there. You also need to realize that Facebook controls access to the people who say they like you. When you post information only a fraction of your followers will ever see that post. Facebook makes a significant chunk of its revenue from promoted posts. You are going to have to pay to reach people, just like pretty much everywhere else. So as important as Facebook and Instagram and Twitter are, you need to make sure that you are paying attention to your website.

First, your website needs to incorporate your neutral branding. I know we sound like a broken record at this point, but the importance of being neutral can't be overstated. It opens so many doors and unifies your community in a way that almost nothing else can. Not everyone who partners with us uses our "Love _____" branding, but by far the majority do because it works. When you partner with us, you get access to everything you need to incorporate your city into that branding.

Second, your website needs to include the basic information that people who know nothing about who you are or what you are doing will want. What day is the event, what will you be doing? Who is behind this organization? Do you have endorsements?

Third, keep it simple. Don't clutter up your site. Make it easy and make it mobile friendly. Most people are going to come to your site from their phones so the site had better work for them or they will be gone.

Fourth and probably most significant, make it as easy as possible for people to sign up to get more information or to sign up for specific projects. Your project leaders are going to need to be able to contact the people who sign up. That means a simple form. Don't ask a lot of questions, at this point you basically need four things: name, what project they are interested in, email, and if possible, a phone number so you can text info to the person. We recommend that you get permission to send that person further information as well. Love Our Cities has a ready-made website platform that handles all of these things for our partner cities.

Presentations

Once your website is up, you are going to want to make presentations to local churches and other organizations, especially to those you are going to be partnering with for projects and for any funding. These presentations are critical because they are going to help you to gain momentum in the community from a visibility standpoint and they will be the primary generator of volunteers. Basically, if they are a group that meets, you need to find a way to talk to them: the rotary club and Kiwanis, PTA or PTOs, Scouts and mother's clubs, churches, city council, the list could go on and on.

This is also one of the reasons why we really recommend having at least three churches represented on your leadership team. There is a built-in connection to make presentations at three, and you work your way out from there. If there are local radio stations or TV, those may be options as well, but they are not as crucial in the first year. Once you have built up some success, they will come to you. You don't necessarily have to have brochures to leave behind, but it helps.

Physical Signage

Chances are you are not going to be able to secure or afford a billboard in year one. That's perfectly ok. You still want and need signs. The simpler the better: "Love _____" with a date works great. You can add your URL, but honestly it will be a bit small and most people will simply Google it anyway. Yard signs are an easy and relatively inexpensive way to get the word out, but we also recommend that you incorporate 4 foot by 8 foot signs as well. A lot of municipalities have pretty strict rules about signs, so you have to do your homework on what is allowed and what isn't. Ideally the churches that your leadership team came from will put them up.

These aren't the only kinds of signs you should be thinking of though. Two of our most important kinds of "signs" aren't signs at all. We do t-shirts and decals every year. You should be wearing a t-shirt when you are doing the presentation and generally it's a good idea to bring a few to give away. Bring lots of decals as well. Later, you may end up selling t-shirts to cover costs, but that doesn't have to happen right away. Both the t-shirts and the decals become an important community branding effort. At Love Modesto, we give decals away to any business or organization that we work with. These often end up on the doors of these businesses. All of this adds up to reinforce your brand and get people excited about what is coming.

Rally Planning

You've got all the big stuff done. Now it's time to plan the rally. This is the culmination of what you have been working toward, it's the party that kicks everything off. You want high energy, enthusiasm and fun. For year one, it's probably not going to be huge. You will need a sound system and probably a small stage or platform so that you can address the crowd, preferably a way to play some music.

If you've got a local coffee shop, see if you can get them to provide coffee. See if you can get a fire truck out for kids to see, bring in the police or the local high school band. There are a lot of different things that you can do to make it fun. The Kiwanis club might do a pancake breakfast, the local hardware store may donate something for a giveaway, radio stations could do a live remote, the possibilities are only limited by your imagination.

Whatever you do, don't make it too long. The whole point is that this is a kick-off for the projects that you will be doing. Thank the people who came and give whatever instructions you need. Give a motivational speech (or find someone who can). We don't recommend letting the politicians like the mayor or the city council people take the mic—it's too easy for a campaign speech to happen. Thank those who are there for their support, acknowledge their help and move on. Often project leaders meet the volunteers working on their projects at the rally, give short instructions and then head off to their respective projects. Some people won't go to the rally, they will go directly to the site. That's ok, but you need to make sure that all of the info is available at the rally.

A Final Thought

It probably all seems a bit overwhelming at this point. That's OK, there's a lot of moving parts. After year one you will add another layer. One successful event is enough to get noticed. It is enough to start developing sponsors. If you are paying attention, you are no doubt noticing costs associated with an event like this. There are, no question. We are going to talk specifically about funding in Chapter 12 but keep this in the back of your mind. The rally can help you to fund what you do. Eventually you will be able to find businesses and organizations who will sponsor you.

One last plug. We have a step-by-step system for all of this. We can walk you through every element and every step along the way. We have partner cities who are more than happy to share what has worked for them and what hasn't worked. Every city who signs up with us gets the support they need to run a successful city-wide volunteer day in year one and the tools to make it even more successful in the following years.

When you have laid a successful groundwork of knowing your community, of listening and learning, of wanting to work with the city and not for it, you will be amazed at what is possible. In fact, your next question is going to be "Now what"?

City Spotlight:
Orangevale/Fair Oaks, California

Year Joined: 2018
City Leader: Brad Squires

Tell us a bit about your city:
Orangevale and Fair Oaks are neighboring towns northeast of Sacramento, California with populations around 30,000 each. Both were established at the turn of the 20th century and are part of unincorporated Sacramento County. Because they are unincorporated, Orangevale and Fair Oaks have no paid city leadership and no designated city budget—everything is managed by the County. What these communities lack in city infrastructure, they make up for in heart and identity. Both communities are made of residents who love the charm and suburban-rural feel of the area. They each have strong small business representation and residents who intentionally shop locally to support them. They each have annual events & traditions which have been in place for over 50 years, and families who look forward to these small-town events every year. Many residents who grew up in Orangevale and Fair Oaks now choose to raise their families there.

What do you love about Orangeville and Fair Oaks, and what are some of the unique challenges you face?
While the charm and identity of Orangevale and Fair Oaks are strong, the unincorporated aspect makes it difficult to maintain schools, parks, roads, and the public spaces in the communities. These two towns compete for dollars across the entire Sacramento County area, which consists of over 1.5 million people. Oftentimes, the unincorporated areas don't have the representation needed to pull together basic maintenance as well as large scale improvements. Nearly all of the civic leaders in Orangevale and

Fair Oaks are volunteers—including the Chamber of Commerce, Rotary clubs, and other service organizations. When the idea about a day of our community coming together in service, it was a great fit and quite well received.

How did you hear about Love Our Cities and how has Love Our Cities helped you?

When we made the decision in 2018 to pursue our first community-wide day of service, our leadership recognized the need for good systems and an online presence to rally the volunteers. Without these types of systems, it is virtually impossible to get the word out and organize projects around the community. It was through a mutual connection with Jeff Kreiser from The ACTS Group that we initially heard about Love Our Cities. We were also introduced to Love Modesto and encouraged to hear about the long, multi-year track record of successful events that they'd pioneered. The resources and templates within the Love Our Cities framework were immensely useful in ramping up the plans for our first Big Day of Service. The tried & true examples of other cities who are also part of the network of community serve days was quite helpful in the initial launch of this first event. Being able to catalog projects, organize volunteer needs, and provide for online signups made the execution and experience of the event very smooth.

Tell us about your city-wide volunteer day and other efforts you have undertaken:

In 2018, an area pastors saw what was happening in one of our neighboring cities through their annual day of service and said, "why don't we do that here?". In Orangevale and Fair Oaks, there are about 25 Christian churches. Most of the leaders of these churches did not know each other on a personal basis at that time, even though many of their buildings are mere miles apart. This pastor and I spoke about the idea of launching a day of service in

Orangevale and Fair Oaks, and I challenged him that if he could get five churches on board, I would take on organizing and leading the event. Within a week, he connected with some of the larger churches' senior leadership and had commitments from them to work together to launch a Big Day of Service. We all gathered and began the planning in January 2018 for a May 5, 2018 event. We met weekly and our leadership team snowballed into over 50 people from local churches, service groups, schools, parks district, and others who helped us pull off the Big Day of Service.

On May 5, 2018, over 1,000 volunteers showed up ready to serve! We kicked off the day with a big rally in the morning complete with our local high school cheer and band groups, special messages from key dignitaries, an opportunity to thank our business sponsors, and a unifying prayer from a group of pastors in the community. Our rally also included a special demonstration of generosity toward a young mother who needed some support from her community. It was a special moment led by our church leaders to do for one person what we hoped to do for many throughout the day: demonstrate abundant love and generosity. We set out to tackle 40 projects ranging from manual work painting and spreading mulch to simple acts of kindness. Our girl scout troops visited senior care facilities to bring cookies, do crafts, and play board games. Volunteers put together care packages to be mailed to overseas military troops. Many of our parks and schools were cleaned up and improved for all to enjoy the weeks and months to follow. It was a heartwarming day that left everyone deeply impacted and really understanding the event's theme - "the power of commUNITY". In 2019, we held our second annual event and it was even bigger and better than our first year. The logistics and planning came together so much easier having completed one event as a team. Most of our project captains and leaders returned, and about half of our projects were repeats from the year prior.

What others are saying:

"Seeing the community come together like it did through the planning & execution of the Big Day of Service is really incredible."

—MaryAnne Povey, Orangevale Chamber of Commerce

"The amount of improvement we saw in our parks in one day was astounding. It's amazing what can be done in one day when a community comes together."

—Lisa Montes, Orangevale Parks Board and Community Leader

"I was looking for ways to serve the community through my business. The Big Day of Service provided a platform for me to donate as well as bring my employees to volunteer to help our community."

—Sean Palmer, Palmer Real Estate

"Through the planning and preparation for the Big Day of Service, we have developed new friendships between our pastors in the community that continue to grow throughout the year"

—Jeff Pitnikoff, Pastor, New Life Community Church

"Our girl scouts look forward to the Big Day of Service every year. In fact, we continue to revisit the senior care homes throughout the year to bring cookies & joy to their residents."

—Jenn Gustafson, Girl Scout Troop Leader in Orangevale

Momentum

Now What?

Here's what you are likely to face after your first event: it's Monday morning, two days after your first city-wide volunteer day. Saturday was great. You accomplished so much for your city in a single day. People came. Projects got accomplished. People had a good time. Even the "fires" were small and easily contained. Yesterday, you were basking in the afterglow. You got shout outs at church and from your friends and supporters, you were riding the high of accomplishment.

No matter where you are on Monday morning, working your regular 9 to 5 or at home or someplace else entirely, here's when it comes crashing in. Reality time. *Now what?* Very few of our partner cities are doing this full time. When you are just starting out, no one is. Yesterday it looked real. Today you are probably second guessing yourself. Most of us do. It's human nature. There's the adrenaline letdown and the second guessing. Did things go as well as they should have? But what about . . .? And then there's the big one, "did we really make a difference?"

And you wonder what's next. (Remember Chapter 3?)

It's natural. I would be more concerned if you didn't have any questions. Even now, over a decade in, we still find ourselves asking questions. Sometimes we even ask the same questions we did at the beginning. But one thing we know for sure, you have reached the tipping point. This morning you are probably mentally and emotionally exhausted, recovering from the weekend. And the questions you are asking right now are probably the right ones. They are more right than you know.

Here's a secret, in many ways it is the key to the future of what you are going to do. You just changed the game in your town. Big or small, whether it was what you dreamed of or not, if you were at all successful then you have changed the game in your town. Almost always the city-wide volunteer day was successful—not perfect, but successful. All the relationships that you have built over the past nine months, all the learning and the partnering, all of the projects and the promotion, all of your planning just proved itself in the eyes of the community. You have become one of the players and it is time to take advantage of the momentum you have just created.

Business and marketing types often refer to the "diffusion of innovation" when talking about the way we as a society embrace things like new ideas and new technology. The basic idea is that 2.5% of people are innovators. If you are reading this book, you may be one. If you just led your first city-wide volunteer day (or if you have ever been the lead person starting a new event or program or ministry or whatever, then congratulations you *are* one). The next group of people are the early adopters. They make up about 13.5 percent of people. And after your successful event, they are paying attention to you.

Maybe you invited five churches in town to participate and you got two or three who joined the leadership team and did a project. Right now, those other churches, plus several more, are no doubt talking in their weekly staff meetings about what just happened over the weekend. "Hey, did you see what happened over the weekend? We had several families who participated in this volunteer day. I went and checked out the rally and it was pretty cool. If they do this again, we should really think about being a part of it."

And it is not just the churches in town who are having discussions. The local nonprofits are either reviewing their project or asking themselves why they didn't participate. The parks department is reshuffling schedules to get to projects that they have put off forever because they don't have to clean up 3 different parks this week. The business community is really paying attention because they saw the people who came out and are wondering how they can leverage that.

You have made the first hurdle and you are on to the next. It's time to use the momentum created by the volunteer day to your advantage.

Celebrate Your Success

Everyone wants to be on a winning team, even if you weren't there. Now is the time to capture all of that positive energy. It starts with celebrating your success. There are all kinds of ways to celebrate, but your goal should be to capture the enthusiasm of the day, give some real-world stats, and encourage people to share their experiences and keep on going. Get stuff out on your social media accounts as soon as you can. Thank people, share photos and encourage others to share them too. People love to let others know when they help. Capitalize on it.

In the first days after your event, honestly on Sunday or Monday if you can, you need to be in touch with the people who participated. Here are a few really practical things that you can do:

First, send an email to everyone who volunteered. Thank them for what they did and let them know what an impact they had. Include pictures from the rally and the projects. Ask them to let you know what they got to be a part of and what happened to them as they participated. We include a survey in this email so that we can capture reactions while everything is fresh in their minds. Ask them to share their stories and pictures on their social media and yours. The more sharing the better. We suggest that you provide a common hashtag as well.

Second, send an email to all of your partner organizations, especially to the ones who sponsored or led projects. Thank them for their participation and all of the hard work that they put in to help your community. Find out what they appreciated and if there is anything that you can do for them. Make sure that you encourage them to connect with the people who volunteered on their project. We have seen repeatedly that the project leaders who do a good job connecting with the volunteers who worked with them retain a lot of those volunteers—and not just for the next city-wide volunteer day.

Third, make sure you connect with leaders from the various sectors in your city. Some of them will be in the group above, some won't. Hopefully though, over the course of the last nine months or so, you have made connections and inroads with many of these people. The successful completion of your first volunteer day will put you on the radar of many who you haven't connected with yet. Now is your chance to reinforce your commitment to and love for your city. When you celebrate the success of what you have done, make sure to thank them for their participation or to invite them to be a part of the next event.

Fourth, make a video for distribution. It doesn't have to be a professional video, but it has to capture the spirit of the event: the rally, the projects, but most importantly the people that participated. It's amazing what can be done on the software that comes installed on a Mac and chances are someone who volunteered can put something together for you in a matter of hours. The video doesn't have to be long, in fact shorter is better—think one to two minutes. Make sure that the churches who participated get a copy to show to their congregations. Ideally, they will show this video the week after the event to keep momentum going. You will also be able to use this video with other groups and throughout the year as you communicate. Put it on your website and your social media.

Fifth, it's time for a press release. Short, to the point, and full of specifics. Include the date, the projects, how many volunteers participated, and the value of the volunteer hours spent (we use www.independentsector.org to calculate the value of the hours). People like to participate in things that they feel are actually accomplishing something. Numbers don't always tell the story, but they help people to frame whether or not something is successful and whether they want to commit the time and energy to be a part of it. Having a few quotes isn't a bad idea either. This shouldn't be long, but if you can show the enthusiasm of the mayor's office and the volunteers, someone who was helped and a partner organization that would be great. Make sure to include a list of organizations who partnered with you. We have lots of experience and can walk you through what to do and when.

One of the challenges here is that the media often wants to do the story the day of the event not after the fact. We make sure to reach out to them in the days leading up to the event and make sure to connect on the day of the event as well. We share stats, make sure that they have great photo and video locations so they can do interviews at the projects, and make sure our leaders are available at the rally too.

And you were wondering what you were going to do in the week after the event. Celebrating success is important for you and for the people who partnered with you. It boosts morale and interest, and it sets the stage for your long-term effectiveness. In a way the event is kind of like a gravitational force, something that pulls people in and keeps them interested. Successfully completing the first event increases that gravitational force, naturally attracting people. So, a part of your communication will be planting the seeds for year two.

Start on Next Year's City-Wide Volunteer Day

That's right, it's time to start thinking about the next one. It's important for your leadership team to have a debrief moment sooner rather than later. You need to think through what happened: what was good, what could have been better? Were there projects that you don't think make sense in the future? Were there others that, in retrospect, you should have included? Chances are that at least one of the people on your team is an analyzer and will have been thinking about these kinds of questions even while the day was happening.

Make sure that you are reaching out beyond your own team. You have spent a lot of time and energy building relationships with people you partnered with. Make sure you are continuing to listen to them. Ask questions, offer encouragement, if a group didn't have the turnout or the success they hoped for, share things that other groups learned so they can get better. The more you continue to work with your partners, the better everyone will get. Depending on your situation it may be beneficial to develop a survey for partner organizations in order to dive deeper into how you can help them accomplish their goals.

As you begin your thinking about your second year, you need to keep three things in mind. These three things will set the path for what you will be working on in the coming months. They are the things that will help you to capitalize on the momentum that you have built and will inform the decisions you make.

Leverage Your Status as Neutral Convener

All of the discussion from chapter six? This is where it pays off for you organizationally. You have just proved to the business and the government, the nonprofits and the churches, that you bring people to the table to get things done for the community. To this point it has been theory, an idea that sounds good but remains unproven. You have just shown everyone that you are a force, in fact you are the hub. You have generated momentum and have shown yourself to be a hub for community engagement. Together you have been able to accomplish something that any one sector or group would not have been able to pull off. Take advantage of the success.

Now is the time to bring people together, to dream bigger and to find out what comes next. What do the schools need from you and your team? Find out what the city government sees as the next big task or threat, see where people are already working and start planning ways to come alongside. The chances of you getting a hearing, of people asking you for help in ways that they didn't even think to ask a week ago, have just skyrocketed. It's time to listen with fresh ears because new opportunities are coming.

Focus on Churches

Remember who you are and where you came from. It will be tempting to focus all of your time and attention elsewhere, but just like Love Modesto, there is a reason you started your leadership team with churches. Remember the common bond and general outlook. Remember too that over 40% of your volunteers came from and will continue to come from churches.

If you don't have a list of all the churches in town (and you should), now is the time. Update what you have. Start contacting everyone to see what they need and how you can be a help to them and find out if they are interested in partnering with you. There will definitely be more interest than there was for year one.

Many churches want to have a direct impact on their communities, but they really don't know how, or they don't have the manpower to be effective. When a church partners with us, they are exponentially increasing their ability to make a positive impact on the community. We tell churches over and over that we can help them reach into the community. We provide entry points for them to be who they are, to do what they want to do. Churches want to increase their impact in the community, and you have just become a leading conduit.

When Love Our Central Coast started, the leadership team was able to get seven churches involved. That's a great starting point. In year two they had fifteen. Now they have over thirty-five churches who are involved. Different churches will be involved in different ways. Some will support you financially. Some will sponsor and run projects. Others will simply send volunteers. All of these levels of support are vital to your long-term success. Spend time talking with the churches in town. Split up the list among your team and start having conversations.

The Sponsors are Coming

The one thing you have probably not thought about a lot to this point is the business community. Take our word for it, they just woke up. If you can motivate a hundred or a thousand people to show up on a Saturday morning for a rally and then to go out into the community, then you can potentially direct those same people towards them.

We aren't talking crass commercialism here or selling your soul, not at all. Think of it this way. It is in the best interests of the businesses in your community for people to care about and invest in your community. In a world of online shopping for virtually everything, increasing local pride and investment matters. Sponsorships can be a lot of different things. The local Starbucks or Duncan Donuts might underwrite coffee for the rally. Local businesses might help underwrite the costs of creating t-shirts for all of the volunteers (your logo on the front and sponsors on the back), and the list goes on. We will talk more about sponsors in chapter 12, but for now, be thinking about sponsors in four ways.

First, financial partners. It costs money to run events and the bigger this gets the more time you or others will have to devote to this endeavor. Your time is valuable, administration has to happen, web sites and mailings, phones—you get the idea—it all costs money. It doesn't have to cost a lot and volunteers are a big part of it, but there are costs. Finding people to help sponsor you financially will be a big help.

Second, advertisers. Some local businesses are going to see you simply as an advertising opportunity. You have to be very careful about this. Don't use the list of volunteers you have developed as a means to sell ad space. Very few things will destroy your credibility as fast as this. At the same time, there are ways to develop mutually beneficial and legitimate partnerships with local businesses. Some businesses are services you will need, and you may well be able to negotiate a discounted price in exchange for advertising.

Third, rally supporters. Whether it is coffee supplied by the local coffee shop (or even McDonalds if you don't have a coffee shop), sponsors of prizes for a raffle, or even donations of microphones and the costs of banners, there are a lot of possibilities.

Fourth, volunteers. Quite often when a business becomes a financial partner or advertiser, they sponsor a project or encourage their employees and family members to volunteer as well. Companies often make their own t-shirts for employees to wear or do drawings for participants. They strengthen employee bonds, becoming a more deeply connected working community.

Sponsors can be a lifeline financially as you build momentum. It takes creativity and a willingness to look for opportunities, but they really do exist, even in small towns. Chapter twelve looks at financing more in depth. We have developed systems to help you take advantage of the opportunities that you don't even know exist yet.

A Bigger Vision

Momentum is really possible at this point. So is inertia. It is possible to think "we've got this" or to be satisfied with what you have accomplished so far, to go into premature maintenance mode and be content with where you are at.

Now is the time to remember why you are doing this in the first place. What doors have opened up since you started? What more did you want to accomplish? What weren't you able to do? The momentum you have gained in the last nine months to a year probably has you thinking bigger. Good!

Now that your first city-wide volunteer day has happened it's time to dream bigger. How do you take the next step? What would it look like if you were able to devote more time and energy to this endeavor? What if you could go full-time?

It is time to start planning for the future. You have laid the groundwork, you have built an engine that is capable of absorbing and storing energy, of releasing it back into your community to make things different.

Here's the thing, a monumental shift is coming. You have changed the landscape in your city, you have gotten people to pay attention. Now they are going to be coming to you. "Can you help us to . . .?" "Can you mobilize people to . . .?" Schools will reach out. The foster agency or the nursing home, the local animal shelter, who knows, but you are going to get calls.

You will be faced with a choice: do we settle for what we have, for refining it and making it run smoother, or do we adopt a bigger vision? And that is part four.

City Spotlight:
Anaheim, California

Year Joined: 2015
City Leader: Nathan Zug

Tell us a bit about your city:
Anaheim was founded in 1857 by a group of German immigrants from the San Francisco area. Located just outside Los Angeles in Orange County, Anaheim is the 10th largest City in California, covering 50 square miles and home to a population of 358,000. We run the gamut from dense urban areas to rolling hills, spacious neighborhoods to condos and townhomes as well as industrial areas. Home to more than 20,000 businesses, we are used to tourists—in a normal year more than 25 million visitors come to visit. Home of the world-famous Disney Resort (the *original* Disneyland), the largest Convention Center on the West Coast and 2 pro sports teams—Los Angeles Angels of Anaheim and Anaheim Ducks—Anaheim also has over 56 parks and 7 school districts. Anaheim has 12 City Departments, including our own Public Utilities Department (water and power) that dates back to the original German founders, that serve racially diverse residents who are well versed in big city life that still retains a family feel.

What do you love about Anaheim, and what are some of the unique challenges you face?
I love the *people* of Anaheim—the diversity, the deep-rooted history and family feel. It is nice to meet residents and visitors from all over the world. Like a lot of California, we have a significant issue with homelessness. We also have aging and densely populated older areas, and the struggle of balancing sports/entertainment/tourism needs and concerns with the needs of residents who actually live in the city.

How did you hear about Love Our Cities and how has Love Our Cities helped you?

I first heard about Love Our Cities from the neighboring City of Fullerton, whose City Leader assisted Anaheim and 5 other nearby cities to launch a "Love Our City" movement in January of 2015. Love our Cities as well as our neighbors at Love Fullerton helped a lot by coaching me along the launch process and helped us to steadily grow over the first few years.

Tell us about your city-wide volunteer day and other efforts you have undertaken:

Due to the sheer size and diversity of Anaheim, we decided to do a 2-location city-wide volunteer day our first year and then 3-5 city-wide volunteer days the second and third years. This structure allowed us to focus on specific areas of the city and develop partnerships in 6 "regions" or Council Districts of Anaheim. Our city-wide volunteer days created a way for people in all roles and areas of the city to give back while at the same time meet needs that existed. Because of our successful multiple city-wide volunteer days each year, Love Anaheim was asked to launch a "pathway to work" program for homeless individuals called Better Way Anaheim. A city funded year-round program, BWA has been highly successful, serving over 1050 homeless individuals to date, inspiring and equipping many to take their next steps towards housing and employment. Additionally, Love Anaheim has launched more than 5, year-round programs to address real needs, offering both a high value for the city and our residents as well as touching the hearts of many who have volunteered since we began in 2016.

What others are saying:

"Love Anaheim's program, Better Way Anaheim, has changed my life – it has given me opportunity and hope."

—Better Way Anaheim Participant

"Love Anaheim has brought schools, businesses and neighborhoods together to successfully serve to meet needs."

—School District Leader

"It has been a positive experience building bridges from the Church to the community."

—Love Anaheim Volunteer

"I have had such a good time volunteering while at the same time doing much needed service to others and making new friends in the process – this has been wonderful."

—Love Anaheim Volunteer

"I wanted to say thank you for your dedicated service to the Anaheim Community. Love Anaheim and Better Way Anaheim have done so much and touched many lives in such a positive way."

—City Leader

Part 4:

Loving Your City Year Round

Y ou have heard our story, you know why how and what we do, you have seen what it takes to make our secret sauce. Here's the monkey wrench.

The one-day city-wide volunteer day is great. It's our unique means of generating community engagement. But let's be clear: if it's all you ever do, you have missed the point entirely. We get the temptation to stay here, to do this one thing well, to be content with this level of success and involvement. But you have to ask yourself: why did we start this thing in the first place?

The answer is simple. You want to make your city different. You want to generate a real change in the lives of real people. You love your city and want it to be a better place.

Love doesn't show up only one day a year.

This may feel like a curveball. "Haven't you told us all along that the one thing that makes you unique is the one-day event?" Absolutely. "Isn't 'all-year' exactly what you said didn't work earlier? I mean, you said you moved from multiple events to one because they were too draining, too exhausting, they were limiting your productivity. What gives?" Glad you asked.

The city-wide volunteer day is the thing that makes us known, brings everyone together, and jump starts community wide engagement. It breaks down barriers and builds bridges. This one event is a catalyst and convener and can expedite relationship building in ways few other things can. This is why we call it the gateway drug to community engagement. It's the best starting point we know. But it's just that, the starting point, not the finish line.

In the final three chapters, we are going to explore what it takes to move from where you are now to reaching your full potential in loving your community. What does it mean to leverage the power of the flywheel you have just created and thereby create systematic change? What would it look like to think differently, to see what *your* city needs from you now and years from now? What would it take to fund a vision like this, to become your own entity?

We believe you can have this kind of lasting impact and we can help you get there. It all starts with a paradigm shift.

Paradigm Shift

No, you did not fix everything with a single event.

No, not everyone knows who you are or what you do.

No, it would not be devastating to the community if you were to go away or if there wasn't a city-wide volunteer day next spring.

But you have made a start. You have built goodwill in the community. You have made a difference in the lives of real people—and not just the ones you helped. You also made a real difference in the lives of those who volunteered. And so now, if you disappeared, people would be saddened. It would leave an empty spot for at least a part of the community.

Love Modesto started with a question. If we left town, just disappeared, would anyone notice? The scary thing for me and my church was that the answer was pretty clear—no, not really. Once you have had your first successful city-wide volunteer day, the answer starts to change. The reality is that it may take more than one. It may be after the repeat success of year two that things will really start to speed up, but the seed has been planted.

In Modesto, we went from "who?" to "wow, that's cool!", to "if Love Modesto goes away our city is in trouble." That's a pretty substantial change. In 1962, physicist Thomas Kuhn wrote a book for scientists that changed the way that almost everyone, not just scientists, think. In *The Structure of Scientific Revolutions*, Kuhn first described a "paradigm shift". "Normal science", Kuhn argued, "is the work that gets done in the framework or paradigm that everyone agrees to. A paradigm shift happens when the way science is getting done bumps up against things that it can't account for". Basically, it means that certain concepts and practices have to change in order to account for what is being observed. This happened in physics when Newton's ideas were updated by Einstein. Kuhn's idea has spread far beyond just science to the realm of wider culture. In fact, we use the term all the time to refer to things like the changes pre and post mass communication, pre and post the internet or even pre and post 9/11.

For Modesto, the paradigm has shifted. In 2008 the city was bumping up against the limits of what was possible. Without a paradigm shift, I really believe that things would have gotten worse, perhaps even much worse, before it got better. Because Big Valley Grace gave us the space to create Love Modesto, because of the things that we have been able to do and become in the decade since, we have forced a paradigm shift. We certainly didn't do it on our own and we certainly wouldn't have predicted what it currently looks like, but it is an indisputable fact that things have changed. Look, we haven't "arrived", we are not the end all and be all, but every year that we exist and work in our city we become a more significant internal cog in our community. If that cog were to be removed there would be a significant impact.

The question, then, is simple: how did we change the paradigm? How do we go from "it would be a bummer if Love Modesto went away" to "we can't do this without them"?

The answer is simple too: love your city year-round.

The one-day city-wide volunteer day became the catalyst for us to become significantly more than just another church or even community event. There are lots of volunteer days in lots of cities around the country. As we outlined in part two, our uniqueness is that we have a base that intentionally seeks to do more than simply have an event. Our foundation of compassion and humility compels us to develop trust and relationships throughout the community and then to champion others. Because we have done this consistently and because we have created a well-run and visible event, the dynamic has changed. The paradigm has shifted. It all starts with a place at the table.

A Place at the Table

The most immediate change that will happen after a successful city-wide volunteer day is that people notice you. Lots of people notice you. The elected and non-elected city government notices you, the schools notice you because of the projects that you have done (chances are in the first year or so you can only do a few and the other schools now want to be a part of this too), businesses notice because people bought supplies for projects and because of all the activity both at the rally and the project sites, churches notice because their people participated in a significant way and of course the nonprofits and other organizations you helped notice.

All of that notice has put you on the map. You are or could be a key piece in potential solutions to community problems because you have shown up as *the* neutral convener in town in a serious way. You are going to be more involved as a group in what goes on in your city—not just for one event but for many events and opportunities. Organizations, maybe even the local government, are going to come to you and ask for your help. As soon as you show the community that you can mobilize people, they are going to want you to help them to do it. "Hey, we are trying to do this thing, can you help? Can you help us get the word out?" They are going to ask you to help them to do what they do.

It is entirely possible to become a regular contributor in your city and for no paradigm shift to occur. You may be facilitating lots of good things once a year, you may be highly respected and even valued in the community, but the test really is whether or not "the way things are" has changed. A paradigm shift in your city requires more than just another person at the table. It requires you embracing your role as a neutral convener and for more than just a single event.

Do not underestimate the value of your place at the table. You are not just another player you have shown that you can bring the players in town together, you can unite them and their causes in a way that probably has never been done before. Paradigm shifts require a fundamental change in thinking, and that starts by asking a simple question.

Who Are We?

Let's be honest, lots of people will look at you and think you are a service organization. They will see the signs and the promotions, even the event and think of you as a group of kindhearted people who do things around your city. There is nothing wrong with service clubs. They are needed in every city and town. But that's not who you are. At this point you are probably not even an "organization" as such, you are a group of people working together who have put together a successful event that pulled together various sectors in your city to work together and accomplish something significant. In a very real sense, you are a force for good in the community. Actually, you are the delivery system for good in the community. Think back to the illustration in Chapter 6—you are the hub.

If you are simply doing a one-day event, it would be reasonable for others to think of you as a service organization in the community. The danger is that you will begin to see yourself this way. We work with lots of cities and there is a tendency, just like in any organization or business, to hit a plateau. You achieve a certain level of success and settle in. You probably don't even realize that you have. Most of us are creatures of habit who default to what we know—yes even those of us who have gone out on a limb to start something new to help our cities. Paradigm shifts can be unsettling. When you are forced to look at things differently there are always consequences. The possibilities for impacting your city will go up, but so will the demands and the cost.

Given the emphasis we have placed on the city-wide volunteer day, it is very easy to look at yourselves as a group of people who come together to put on an event to do good in your city once a year. All of this talk of a paradigm shift might seem like it is exactly the opposite of what we have been saying thus far. It's really not opposite at all. Embracing the paradigm shift means that you see the city-wide volunteer day for what it truly is—an engine that can drive significant, sustainable, and long-term results in a way that few things can. We have used various metaphors for it—secret sauce, flywheel, engine. All of them point to a simple truth: the city-wide volunteer day is the part that brings people in, that galvanizes and sets direction, but truly it is a means not an end. In business, the product a company makes or sells does so to solve a problem in a unique way. The same is true for the city-wide volunteer day. It brings people together, it provides energy, it enables the possibility for the paradigm shift of loving your city year-round.

Change and growth will always be a part of leading an organization. During the middle of writing this book, our organization continued to evolve. We are now two separate entities: Love Our Cities is the name of the national organization and Love Stanislaus County is the name of our local organization. Love Modesto is still the name of our event, but because of the ongoing work we do beyond our city limits we needed to shift our name to include the whole county. We work with lots of different cities who are at various stages on their journey. Some have just started; some have been doing this for years and are still at a fairly small footprint. Some cities have started with a bang, grew and then fizzled out because they were basically a one person show then something happened to that one person. Several of those cities have come back after a year or two with new leadership. That new leadership is quite often better positioned to navigate the paradigm shift.

I bring this up because it is important to realize that navigating the paradigm shift is going to take a strong leadership team. It will mean thinking differently about who you are as a group, and possibly as an organization. At this point you are running on purely volunteer staff. You all have jobs and families and lives and as important as this is, there are capacity issues, right? This is a real issue that you are going to face.

Making the shift from a one-day event to a year-round identity is not small and it is not without its challenges. It will require more time and more investment in people. It will require that you make sure that as a team you are thinking about who you are and what it means to be the hub of community engagement in your city.

Put all of this together and you are going to have some significant questions to ask as a team. Who are you? Who can you be? What does it look like to love your city year-round? These are important questions that you will have to wrestle with. We help our partner cities do just that, ask, wrestle with these questions, but in the end, they have to figure it out. They have to own what it means in their city. The heartbeat is the same, but the way it plays out will necessarily be different. Being the neutral convener for the town will look different depending on several factors. Things like the size of your city, the kinds of needs you have, the available resources and people will all play into this. There is no question that bigger cities have greater ability to generate more momentum and do so more quickly. That doesn't mean a group in a smaller city can't have a significant impact, we have seen it happen.

The city of Madera, California is a great example. A city of around 60,000, Madera is a small to medium size city (on the small end in California, but maybe not so small in other areas of the country). Madera has been a partner city for a while, but they were on the verge of dying because there was one person from a single church doing most of the heavy lifting. Great guy, doing great things, but he had a full-time job and he was simply not able to do everything needed to keep things moving. To his credit, he kept things going for a couple of years until someone else could take over. April was a mom, a volunteer at the church without an official role at the church. She stepped up, took over and has been doing a great job. She got a bunch of churches on board and now works through a ministerium in town, not just one church. She has spearheaded things with the police department and has done a lot of work to help clean up the river in town. She has rallied the troops in town and has helped to make the transition to year-round thinking.

Once, a bunch of us were on a call talking about various things including funding and April made a comment that she didn't need more funding (nice problem to have, right?). What was beautiful was how the other cities pushed her. "Do you want to do this full-time?" "Are you passionate about this? "You need to get sponsors so you can spend more time and effort building a team and doing things." A lightbulb went off in her head. She wasn't seeing things that way yet. She had done an amazing job, she started to get things moving toward loving her city year-round, but it was pretty limited. The other cities coming together helped her to see something she had not before. Together they helped her see that she had moved things in her city, she could think bigger and do more.

Think Bigger and Go Deeper

Some, like April, are go getters, but they need someone to show them what they have done and what the possibilities are. Not everyone can handle the transition of thinking bigger and going deeper. That's not a slam on them in any way. Different people are different. This is one of the reasons we really believe in having a leadership team and not simply relying on one person or one church to do everything. It's not the only reason, but it is significant. When we work together to share a vision, greater things can happen, someone else's strengths can cover for my weaknesses and vice versa.

The reality is that there is always more we can do. There is always another need, another great cause. When you start thinking about loving your city year-round those needs will seem to multiply in front of your eyes. The thing is, it is going to happen whether you like it or not, whether you ask or not. It will happen on your very first volunteer day. It did for Love Modesto. One of the principals at a local elementary school was very appreciative of the project that we did—cleaning up graffiti or working on the playground—but she told us that if we really wanted to make a difference in the lives of the kids there, they needed mentors. It was a school with very little parental involvement, lots of broken homes, lots of people struggling to make ends meet. Often the parents had to be away to work. The principal saw the consequences firsthand every day. Kids were drifting, they needed positive role models in their lives. We would have never known of the need or seen the opportunity without the volunteer day, but on its own it can't do that job. The people who volunteered? They can.

At a retreat with city leaders from across the country, I was asked if I would rather have 1,000 cities with just a volunteer day or 100 cities with a sustainable model in place for the year. I didn't hesitate, 100 all day long. Don't get me wrong, over the next 10 years it's our dream to work with 1,000 cities around the world and to help them make sure they have a sustainable model for loving their cities. That's the paradigm shift. How do you leverage what you were able to accomplish in your one-day event so that you can love your city year-round? It may mean new people on the team. It may mean that you shift what you have been as a group and you become your own nonprofit so that you can dedicate more resources. It doesn't have to be bigger to be bigger, but it does need to be a mindset that is bigger than a single day.

When you start to think this way, you can start to really dive into what your city needs.

City Spotlight:
Fullerton, California

Year Joined: 2014
City Leader: Jay Williams

Tell us a bit about your city:
Originally known for its Valencia Orange groves, and more recently as the birthplace of the electric guitar because of Leo Fender, Fullerton is now known as the Education Community. Founded in 1887, the city is named after George Fullerton, the Santa Fe Railway agent who brought the railway through the city. About 25 miles southeast of downtown LA, the current population is about 143,000 and it is a very diverse city.

I see Fullerton as a unique city in Orange County. I often say it's the center of the kingdom of God. I know that's not true, but if you pay attention and explore outside of your neighborhood, you find our city saturated with God's presence. Before Fullerton, I never lived in a city where there was the other side of the tracks. Fullerton is divided into two, north and south. North Fullerton is more affluent with better roads, more green space, and better access to amenities. South Fullerton often receives the least care and has higher crime rates, and it started with redlining, a practice where people of color were only allowed to rent and purchase homes in an identified area of south Fullerton. However, south Fullerton is flourishing with generous people who are gracious and hospitable.

What do you love about Fullerton, and what are some of the unique challenges you face?
I've learned more about the goodness of God in south Fullerton than anywhere else in the world. One of Fullerton's greatest gifts

is south Fullerton, and we are blessed with some great people and organizations that are amplifying the voices and gifts our neighbors have to share. OC United, Solidarity, Joya Scholars, Cal. State Fullerton, Habitat for Humanity, St. Jude Hospital, and the Fullerton Collaborative all collaborate and come alongside our neighbors to help them flourish. As a result, Fullerton is thriving and moving towards a more united city where the railroad tracks no longer serve as a dividing line.

I have been blessed to see non-profits, churches, city government, schools, businesses, and residents work together and are building trusting relationships to address our cities biggest problems. Homelessness, education, human trafficking, poverty, immigration, justice, and healthy and whole life are all being addressed in collaboration.

During COVID, the collaborative relationships that were cultivated for years began to bear fruit that brought a larger, more diverse group into God's mission in Fullerton. Those relationships and collaboration are what make Fullerton unique. More and more people are figuring out God is on the move in their city, and they get to come along for the ride.

How did you hear about Love Our Cities and how has Love Our Cities helped you?

For years I led city-wide serve days as a part of one large church doing good works "for the city." Then one summer we painted the exterior of a historic building for a local women's shelter in partnership with two other churches and our local police department. It was so fun I determined to never do another serve day alone. I went on a search to find a web-based volunteer management system that would help me organize such a collaborative multi-church effort. A friend whom I had worked with before had moved to Stockton, California and was leading a large city-wide movement. She told me that their city was now participating with Love Our Cites and had begun Love Stockton. I began to read all about the Love Modesto mission, vision, and story and realized this was exactly what I was looking for. In fact, their website program was the same program we had used in a multi-church network in Southern California years before. But even more important than the website, the idea of everyone (churches, businesses, schools, NPO's, service organizations, and local residents) coming to the table to work "with the city" captured my heart even more. I was completely hooked when I recognized that our annual big event could be a catalyst for serving the other 364 days of the year. I gathered a team of strategic leaders from our city, shared the vision for what Love Fullerton could look like, and quickly they were all in agreement. Next, I went to our network of church leaders and shared the vision, they all said they were on board and signed up as well. Finally, I reached out to our city's Chief of Police and invited him to take a road trip with me so we could see Love Modesto in person. Over the two-day trip we formed a friendship and began to dream together. We talked about the possibilities the whole way up and back. Seeing Love Modesto pull off their big rally was so exciting it filled us with vision to bring that energy with us back to our city.

Tell us about your city-wide volunteer day and other efforts you have undertaken:

We had our first Love Fullerton City Wide Serve day in May of 2014 with about 2000 volunteers and probably 20 participating churches. The city-wide volunteer day quickly became a catalyst in North Orange County. Fullerton's Chief of Police began to tell our city's story whenever he met with the other local police departments, and pretty soon they were all asking for City serve days in their city. Within a few years, there were 10 surrounding North

Orange County cities all offering City Serve Days and joining us on the same day. OC United, the NPO that runs Love Fullerton began to grow and expand our reach and impact after our first big event. We have been very intentional about impacting our city during the other 364 days of the year with our initiatives focused on homelessness, foster care, domestic abuse and under-resourced neighborhoods. Our mission is to empower individuals, families and communities through restorative relationships and whole person care. Our vision is to see everyone safe, connected and whole.

What others are saying:

"This was my son and I's 3rd year participating. It was by far the most organized this event has ever been, and twice as fun! Can't wait for next year!"

"The most important lesson I learned was that things ran smoothly because I took time to get to know my volunteers a bit beforehand, and everyone had an assigned task before they got there that they were comfortable doing. I wanted it to be a great experience for both the volunteers and our guests, and that is exactly what happened! God is GREAT!"

"I serve because it allows me to meet my neighbors, love my neighbors, and make a difference in my community."

"Our project leader was incredible. I'm not a church person, but he talked to me about why he helps out on projects through Love Fullerton and now I plan on visiting his church. If people like him are real— I want to be a part of whatever he has."

What Does Your City Need?

"What counts in life is not the mere fact that we have lived. It is what difference we have made to the lives of others that will determine the significance of the life we lead."

— Nelson Mandela

What does *your* city need? Some things are fairly universal—chances are there is a park or other public space that could use cleaning up every spring, schools always need help, nursing homes can use people to come and visit with shut in patients. There are lots of things that transcend location. But there are other things that are unique to your city. What are they?

If I asked you to write down a list of things that you would like to do in a city-wide volunteer day, some of them would fall into the general category, but at least a few would no doubt be unique to your city. As you listen and learn, as you plan and find projects for your first city-wide volunteer day you will gain a lot of insight into your town. You will no doubt learn things that you simply didn't know before. You built that into the partnerships you formed and the projects that you worked on. The next step is to refine what you brought into the city-wide volunteer day by learning from what came out of it. Now is the time to take the next step in meeting the needs of your city.

Leverage Your Momentum

One of the key take-aways from Part Two was having an attitude that there is always something more to learn, something that we can do better. A humble attitude is by definition one that does not think that we have all the answers. The very first way to leverage the momentum of your city-wide volunteer day is to learn everything you can about what happened. Hearing from volunteers is always important, but the place to begin is with the project leaders.

Not every project leader is created equal, but all are important and can give you vital information. These are people who are committed to their cause and your community, they are the ones who volunteered not only to do but to lead others in a hands-on way. Think of them as giving you information from the front lines. Find out every bit of information about the project that you can—what worked, what didn't work, how many people were there, what could be done better, was there something that should have been done but wasn't? These types of questions and more will help you to refine the event for the next year, but not only that, it will give you greater insights into the specific needs of your city. The insights you gain may be seemingly small— "you know, there was a lot of trash at this one end of the park. There were no lights over there and only one trash can. I bet if another trash can was added and a light was put up by it then there would be less of a problem." Then again, the insight may be pretty large—like when the principal told us about needing mentors.

Taking time to dialogue with the project leaders is an important first step in leveraging your momentum. Like we mentioned in Chapter Nine, the faster you can get to them the better. Let's face it, memories and ideas fade faster than we would like to admit. If you can, have a survey ready to go *before* the volunteer day and send it out to the project leaders within a few days of the event. Ask the questions I mentioned above and any others that will help you hear about the specifics of your city. Make sure that you leave space for the project leaders to write in their ideas for improvement. You probably won't be able to do everything that you hear and perhaps some of the ideas won't be practical, but getting the information is important. It also reminds the leaders that you care about them. It will be an encouragement to them and will reinforce the value of what they do. Surveys alone aren't enough, though. It's hard to convey passion in an email and sometimes the very act of having a conversation sparks a memory or an idea that you would not have gotten otherwise. We will come back to the project leaders in a moment.

It is also a good idea to connect directly with the volunteers as well. Capturing their experiences and enthusiasm is a great way to let others know how much of an impact the volunteer day has. It also can lead to great endorsements for future events and maybe even future project leaders and ideas. Remember, you are gathering information at this point as well as building more trusting relationships in your community. That information is definitely valuable as you talk to leaders from other sectors, and it may lead to significant new endeavors.

Of course that is the next step. Have discussions with other leaders in your city. Take what you learned from your event and from the follow up conversations you had with project leaders and volunteers and start dialogues. Don't charge in with all the answers, instead let people know what you have learned, ask more questions, "hey, we did a survey of project leaders and heard this, our volunteers told us this, what do you think? Does that make sense? How can we partner with you to do a better job next year?"

Leveraging your momentum is going to mean more conversations with the leaders of the various sectors in your city, not less. You have started to earn the right to be heard and now leaders from those sectors are much more likely to decide that they should collaborate with you. They will think of things that they hadn't before. They are likely to bring up larger and systemic issues that you hadn't thought of. This is the part where you listen for the kinds of ongoing needs that your city is facing.

Where are the points of crisis and discomfort? What would the city or the nonprofit do if resources weren't an issue? Is there an underlying reality that can be addressed?

Universal or Unique

One of the trickiest aspects of leading the charge for community engagement is assessing what the needs of your city really are. We have spent a lot of time listening and learning that every city is dealing with issues that are common to virtually everyone, as well as issues that are unique to that particular city. It really isn't an either/or situation. It's a both/and situation. It is crucial to keep this in mind as you seek to love your city year-round.

It is all too easy to universalize everything on the one hand or think that you are entirely unique on the other hand. We do it with people and we do it with cities. We fall into the trap of thinking "well if this was the issue in that city, it is the issue in ours too" or "you have no idea what it is like in our town, no one else is dealing with _____." The truth lies somewhere in-between. There are universal issues that all of us, and that every city deals with. The way those issues show up, though, can be very unique.

Take Palo Alto and East Palo Alto California as an example. Separated by a freeway, these two cities lie in-between San Jose and San Francisco. East Palo Alto is actually closer to the water and a little north of Palo Alto. You would think that their issues would be very, very similar. It only stands to reason: same area of the country, next door neighbors, shouldn't what works in one work in the other? You might think this, but you would be wrong.

Palo Alto is one of the highest earning demographics in the country from a zip code perspective. East Palo Alto is quite poor. As of a few years ago, drugs and violent crime made up a disproportionate cause of death in East Palo Alto. These were not really an issue for Palo Alto. You know what was? Teen suicide. Kids in one of the highest income brackets in the country and they don't know what they have to live for. Right next door to a place where gangs and violent crime are a day-to-day reality. What you do to help in one place simply will not be the same, it cannot be the same, as what you do in the city literally next door. No, someone could argue that there is a universal at work here—disaffected youth in our individualized and largely affluent culture. I'm not sure and don't pretend to be, because I am not a sociologist or a psychologist. But that universal cannot be treated in an identical way if you want to help solve a problem. Sure, you have to show young people that their lives matter, but you can't do it the same way for the kid with nothing, who can make more money in a day on the street than his mother makes in a week, and for the kid who lives in the multimillion-dollar house. It just doesn't work.

If you stop to think about it, you realize that this example is not as extreme as it seems at first glance. Think about your city. Think about the one next door, or 20 miles away. Are the issues identical? Chances are they are not. There may be common threads, common kinds of issues, but the way that they work themselves out will be very different. Part of your job is to listen and learn so that you can tailor the things that you do to your city. You have to go into the process thinking about things in those terms. One of the things we talked about when we started thinking about this book was the idea of "principles not practices".

Sometimes in books like these, you hear an author saying, in effect, "if you just do these 10 things then you too can have these superfantastic results!" Honestly, they sound like infomercials. You and I know better. The things that work in one place will not necessarily work somewhere else. The principle here, when it comes to loving your city year-round, is to pay attention to what you are hearing, to what you are seeing. How do the issues of the day uniquely work themselves out in your city? If you try a generic one-size fits all approach you will ultimately fail. Some things work that way. You might even get a ways down the road, but you won't be able to function as the neutral convener in your city the way you want to because you aren't really paying attention to its specific needs. You are kind of like my group that tried to clean up the neighborhood without local buy-in. It looks good for a few days, but a week later you don't even know anything happened.

Get Behind or Get Building

There is an equal and opposite problem to the generic solutions problem, you may have heard of it: NIH Syndrome. As in "not invented here." Sometimes we think that the best thing to do is to start our own thing. Start a bunch of our own things because we see the needs and therefore the solutions. This can be especially tempting for someone in our shoes, and even more tempting when you make the shift to loving your city year-round. you have had success in creating an event that got people engaged, you want to solve problems. If it worked once, why wouldn't it work again? After all, aren't we the neutral convener in town? If we want to love our city year-round and we are the ones who know what the issues are and how to get people engaged, let's just start a bunch of things that are tailored to our community.

Here's the thing, if you have been doing your job well, if you have been paying attention and listening at all, chances are you do know things and see things that others aren't seeing. Chances are, though, starting something brand new is not entirely or maybe even mostly the answer. Now is the time when you really have to guard against NIH Syndrome. It breeds in the fertile soil of modest success. It plays on your ego and makes you forget the thing that got you here—championing others. When you started working toward your very first city-wide volunteer day, you listened and learned, you found out who was doing things in town, and you drew attention to what they were doing. You got them on the list of projects, and you let others know.

But that is only step one in championing others. You drew attention to what was going on. You let others know that they could get involved and gave them a way to do so. The next step is to truly collaborate with those organizations for long-term results. The temptation to start your own thing is real. Sometimes you will need to create something new, but the danger of creating silos looms very large. Our job is to first come alongside those who are already doing things and empower them, to help them do what they do more effectively and better. We think of it this way: we are the bridge, the supply line. We are not always the solution on the front lines, we provide resources so that the people on the front lines can do their job. Those resources might be volunteers or awareness or know-how or any number of things, but it starts with true collaboration with the people on the front lines.

Who are the organizations you worked with to get projects on the docket for your first city-wide volunteer day? What are their ongoing needs? What are the issues that they face on a day-to-day basis? What would it look like for you to help them? How do you come alongside and get behind what is already happening? Back in chapter nine we talked about following up with the project leaders and helping them to reach out to the people who volunteered for their projects. This is important on a very practical level *for them*. We have seen over and over that when a project leader does a good job of connecting with the volunteers they worked with, they will get some of those volunteers to do more than just the one-day event. One of the biggest needs of most nonprofits is volunteers. You have created a bridge to these groups with the city-wide volunteer day. Now is the time to use the bridge.

You have contact information from a group of people who have told you that they love their city. A group of people who have said that they want to help. Use it. Of course, you have to be careful. Don't spam people. Don't become a nuisance. But you can inform people. You can let them know about the needs and the ongoing opportunities in your city. Use your social media platforms to get behind the things that your partner organizations are doing. You may be surprised at what comes your way when you do.

One of the reasons we recently changed our name to Love Stanislaus County from Love Modesto is that we were asked to be a part of an ongoing county-wide initiative. One of the things that the county realized was that they were spending a huge percentage of their yearly budget on welfare related expenses. If they could spend some of the money on prevention, that would, in the long run, have a far better effectiveness for everyone. The county contracted with the United Way to run a lot of the programs. The United Way is good at doing a lot of things, but the one piece that the county wanted to develop was community engagement. Because we have worked together over the years, because we have developed a reputation for mobilizing people, the United Way came to us and said, "Hey, you know how to connect with people really effectively, can you help us to make the connections?" Because of our collaborations, we have been able to become the forward face of what the United Way is accomplishing, and it is all in alignment with what the county is doing. In this case we were both getting behind what was already going on as well as building something new.

More often than not, the issues your city faces are being addressed in some way, shape, or fashion, the trick is finding out about it. But sometimes the reality is there are things falling through the cracks. Things that the county or the city or the nonprofits haven't been able to address or can't address due to red tape or whatever. Sometimes they simply don't know what to do. Because of the relationships that we have built within our community, because we have mobilized volunteers and have built a reputation for helping other organizations, now they are coming to us and saying "look we have a problem, an issue that we can't deal with. Can you help?" This is where all of the hard work that we have put in over the years pays off. We have the knowledge and the connections as the neutral convener to help and to start things that are specifically needed in our community.

Meeting Ongoing Needs: Love Modesto Stories

As Love Modesto grew, and as we became known as the neutral convener in our city, we would not only hear about the needs and the issues of the city, but we were also increasingly asked to get involved. We also began to see just where there were cracks in the system, places where there were gaps that weren't quite being filled. These cracks are different in every city, but they almost always exist, and this is where your expertise in loving your city allows you to build something new using the contacts, relationships and expertise that you have already developed. In Modesto we identified three specific areas: kids in the foster care system, neighborhoods, and schools. Other places have a different set of needs. Our partners in Fullerton, CA have identified families, neighborhood schools, homelessness and seniors. Your city will have its own list.

We want to be really crystal clear here, Modesto's issues may or may not be yours. The principle here is that we learned about these things by sitting down with others, by developing real relationships with people on the front lines, learning the needs and the struggles in our community and by helping them do what they do. The more that we did this the more opportunities we got to help, the more we developed expertise that allowed us to get behind what was happening and to build solutions where there weren't any. We know we sound like a broken record at this point, but we just can't say it enough, these are the things that open the doors so that we could help. Don't take these examples as "this is the next step and you need to add them to your city-wide volunteer day." Instead, think of them as the kind of thing that you could do as you love your city year-round. Your list will probably be different, but hopefully these examples will inspire you with possibilities.

We started three focused year-round initiatives under the Love Modesto banner. Realize that this is not an overnight thing. We have had fits and starts, we have had successes and failures. Rather than go into detail for each, here's a snapshot of the first two (you can find more details on the individual websites for each program) and then we will look at the third as a sort of case study in what a focused, ongoing initiative to address the ongoing need of your city might look like.

Love Our Neighbors

Love Our Neighbors (www.loveourneighbors.org) connects the people in our community to the ongoing needs in our community. Just like we make it easy for people to sign up for the city-wide volunteer day, Love Our Neighbors makes it easy to volunteer or donate to ongoing needs.

Our website hosts donation opportunities for several other organizations as well as a sign-up form for volunteering. Through it, we are able to directly and concretely help our community to meet the ongoing needs of our neighbors.

Love Our Schools

Love Our Schools (www.loveourschools.com) was born out of those two principals coming to me, independent of one another, and saying "thanks for all of the help, it was great, but we need positive role models. Our kids need people who invest in them, who tell them that they are proud of them." It has taken us a while to get there, but we are finally getting traction. Love Our Schools offers:

- training and coaching to educators so that they can build sustainable partnerships with students, parents, business, faith communities, and other community members
- asset mapping so that educators and their partners know what is available in their area
- strategic community engagement planning
- coordinating and co-facilitating catalyst events to increase partnership

Love All of Our Kids

One of the really big needs in our area is the foster system. You name it there is a need because there are around 800 kids in and out of the system at any given time. This isn't just a Modesto issue of course—in California alone there are about 60,000 kids who need a home. Sometimes it's for a short time and sometimes it's for a lifetime. The need is significant, and the system was simply not able to keep up with all the needs. As we became more and more familiar with the needs in the community, it became pretty clear that we could help to mobilize people and fill in some of the gaps. There were three pretty obvious ways that people could help and one that wasn't on anyone's radar until we stumbled on it.

With as many kids in the system as there are, you can guess the first way that people can get involved: fostering and adoption. Bottom line there simply aren't enough places to go around for kids who need homes. Second, people can donate time. From spending time teaching teens in the system a skill, to advocating for the best interests of foster kids in the court system, to being a camp counselor or even being a mentor mom or grandmother to young moms who are in the system, there are a lot of ways that people who aren't able to foster or adopt can help people in need. Third, there is always a need for items to help out. When a family enters the system there is usually a crisis of one kind or another. Things like household items, furniture or even groceries can be a big help. We added a page to our Love Modesto site to make it easy for people to see and understand the needs and to get involved tangibly.

As my wife and I got more involved in the foster care world personally, we went to a conference to learn more. There was a county on the East Coast somewhere, I honestly don't remember where anymore, but anyway some people went to the county and asked a simple question "what can we do to help?" The needs there were not totally unlike ours. There were a lot of kids in the system and in transition. Sometimes things go wrong with a placement—there are lots of reasons, but often kids are taken out of a bad or difficult situation with almost no warning. The kids basically couldn't take anything with them—because they didn't own anything. Together they came up with the idea of creating a little kit that was age and gender appropriate that could be given to the kids in these situations as they have to be removed from whatever the situation is.

We thought it was a great idea. When we got back home, we connected with one of the people in social services in the county. We had a conversation. We asked if there was anything we could do to help and we said "hey, we were just at this conference and we heard about this idea that some people are doing out East. Would something like this work here?" We didn't tell him what to do. We didn't come in with solutions, we asked questions to see what we could do. They thought it was a great idea, but they wanted to start small, to see how it would go. So we did.

We found someone who could volunteer to coordinate putting together what we called "comfort kits" for these kids. We did start small: she put together backpacks with some basic things for the kids—toothbrush, pillow, a book, teddy bear, that kind of thing—in her garage. Maybe 40 or so. It was a great success. The next year we did more because a MOPS (Mothers of Preschoolers) group got involved and the year after that a high school in town did it. But it was low key, word of mouth, mainly people from our church. The community didn't know about it. Sound familiar?

So I saw this thing happening, we had a volunteer running it, it was a great thing, but it was taking up a lot of our time and resources, it wasn't really the kind of thing that we did—it was the kind of thing that we helped others do. But it was a real need that wasn't being filled otherwise. It dawned on us that we are really good at events. What if we made an event out of comfort kits in December? What if we got people to come out and put these things together as groups or families or whatever? So we did. For four years now in the first week of December we have a Christmas Comfort Kit Drive. Our team now leads a rally at a center of our city location on a Saturday morning, there's food and music and our volunteer who started this thing gets to present and let people know of the need. And guess what, the event gets people to see the ongoing, year-round needs related to foster care. The Comfort Kit Drive helps to recruit volunteers to help and gets these kits into the hands that need them. For the past four years we have been about to do over 1,000 kits a year. We don't need all of them in our county (thankfully!), so we have been able to coordinate with over fifteen other counties around California.

Love All Our Kids (www.loveallourkids.com) now has two staff people who oversee all of this stuff. In many ways, Love All Our Kids does the same things that Love Modesto does but in a very focused way. We work with others to help them do what they do more effectively, and it helps us to love our city more.

Concluding Thoughts

When the paradigm shift hits you, when you start to leverage your momentum, you can truly start to love your city year-round. The possibilities will start opening up and the opportunities will get bigger and bigger. It's exciting and can be more than a little overwhelming. More likely than not there is a little voice in the back of your head saying, wait a minute, this is a full-time job and then some.

How does this all get done? Who pays for it all? Glad you asked! For starters, we help cities across the country start exactly these kinds of initiatives. We can even help you understand how to make them financially viable. As for general funding questions, that's chapter 12.

City Spotlight:
Florence, South Carolina

Year joined: 2016
City Leader: Chris Handley

Tell us a bit about your city:
Florence began as railway station and inn in the mid 1800's though it was not chartered until the 1880's. It has remained an important transportation hub even after the rail became less important. Interstates 95 and 20 converge in Florence making it a great location for overnight lodging as people travel up and down the east coast from Miami to New York.

Florence is a city of influence in the north eastern corner of South Carolina. With a population of about 45,000 and a metro area of about 150,000, it is the most populated community in that region. It has the largest medical system in the ten-county region of the state, as well as several national corporations including General Electric, Otis Elevator, and Riuz Foods. Recently the city of Florence made history by electing its first African American woman as mayor.

What do you love about Florence, and what are some of the unique challenges you face?
Florence and our surrounding communities are multi-ethnic! This is both beautiful and challenging. About 50% of the population is white and 46% is African American. Racism is certainly something that must be addressed in our community, but it is wonderful how black and white alike are trying to work together to improve this community! Yes, we deal with staple issues such as drugs, sex trafficking, gangs, racism and poverty. But there is also a spirit of collaboration in Florence. For example, there is a group

of pastors that has an equal number of black and white that meet together monthly.

How did you hear about Love Our Cities and how has Love Our Cities helped you?

Helping Florence Flourish first heard of Love Our Cities through a consultant and author Glenn Barth. Part of his work is pointing local groups to best practices from around the country. Love Our Cities was an organization he recommended. Helping Florence Flourish had a dream to launch a season of service in our community like the Serve Days that Love Our Cities already had established. Jeff and his team provided the technological support as well as the inspiration and best practices to get our efforts better organized. The collaboration that Love Our Cities affords groups like HFF is invaluable: the Leader's Forums have allowed us to listen to other organizations and learn how they were thinking and planning. This cross pollination is making a difference for Helping Florence Flourish.

Tell us about your city-wide volunteer day and other efforts you have undertaken

HFF began work in Florence in June of 2016 with service projects over a two-week period that we call ServeFLO. We have helped with small repairs on homes; painted schools inside and out and upgraded gardens around the buildings. Several non-profits have benefitted from teams doing repair and gardening around their facilities. The City of Florence has asked us to work in city parks and do trash pick-up in distressed areas. We continue to build good will in the community. An important aspect of our work is addressing racial tensions and our desire to pull the races together. One of the ways we do this is by bringing blacks and whites together on our service project teams.

Because of HFF's service to the community and the reputation we have developed, the city's local Senior Citizens Association Center asked HFF to step in during the early COVID days to deliver the meals on wheels to senior adults. This happened during a critical period where the Center had lost many of their volunteer helpers because they were in high-risk categories for contracting COVID themselves. HFF was able to provide volunteers for the two-month period to assure that the Center's meal recipients got their meals as planned.

Our next work Season of Service will be a building project that helps a local homeless ministry build a Tiny House campus. These 250 square foot homes will temporarily house homeless families as they move through a program to get them back on their feet. Additionally, a newly elected city council woman and friend of HFF contacted us to begin planning a Serve Day that the city wants to coordinate with all churches, nonprofits and business partners in 2021. Our past work has been an inspiration for this initiative, and we look forward to how this will continue to build the Kingdom.

What others are saying:
"Thank you and your team for making our school look better!"

"The neighborhood has been blessed to have the ServeFLO team cleaning up and cooking out for the community. Many thanks!"

"I love being involved in my community and seeing the ways we can all help and come together."

If You Build It, the Funding Will Come

"Life's most persistent and urgent question is:
'What are you doing for others?'"
— **Martin Luther King, Jr.**

Here we are at the end and we are just now getting to funding. No doubt some of you have skipped ahead to this chapter. We get it. A lot of the stuff that we have talked about doesn't cost you anything but time and effort, but the reality is, time and effort aren't free, and neither are things like office supplies and signs and phones and, well you get the picture. Doing things well is going to take some money. When you start out, you really don't need a lot of money to get a city-wide volunteer day off the ground. As you grow and start doing more, especially when you start loving your city year-round, it will take more.

Eric here, whether we like it or not (and let's be honest, for most of us it's decidedly in the "not" category), funding means fundraising (Jeff calls it vision casting and he has a point). Fundraising for your new venture in loving your city can be a tricky adventure. The reality is, especially when starting out, leaders can spend a significant amount of time fundraising throughout the year, which can be demoralizing for someone who "just wanted to do something to help my city!" Fundraising just doesn't feel like it is what you signed up for, does it? Yet, with the right mindset, fundraising can help build momentum, increase participation from the community, as well as finance your operations.

This chapter is going to be a crash course intro into the world of fundraising—at least the way we do it. It is not a magic bullet, and we aren't going to be able to answer every question you have. What we will do is give you a 10,000-foot view of an approach that has proven itself successful for us and for many of the cities that we work with. It all starts with a specific mindset that most people have about money.

A Stake in the Game

It's not really a secret—people put their money into what they care about. It doesn't matter if its houses or cars or education or church or recreation or supporting causes. People don't spend money on things that they don't care about, at least most people don't. When it comes to any charity, any nonprofit—and that is the way that people are likely to look at you even if you don't have a separate entity—people support you because they believe in you and what you do.

Way back in chapter 8 we talked about creating a leadership team from at least three congregations in town. Part of the reason for this is splitting up the responsibilities and part of the reason is to generate a solid base for funding in your first few years. Depending on the size of your city, the total cost for your first city-wide volunteer day may be in the range of $5,000. Your very first ask is going to be to the churches where your leadership came from. Hey, we are getting this started, and we need you to put in X dollars. How you divide that amount up is going to depend on your situation. Some churches are going to have more money available than others; size is going to be a factor. These are all logistics that you are going to have to work out, but you are looking for skin in the game. When a church is actually putting their money toward this, they are going to be more invested. And that is what you are ultimately looking for.

The first year you are looking to seed the event. The principle of having a stake in the game never changes. There's an important flip side to the principle of having a stake in the game—whoever funds a thing owns that thing. This is another reason why we really recommend having multiple congregations involved from the beginning. We will go over multiple funding streams in a bit, but from the start you need a mindset that seeks to have as broad of a funding base as possible. When you do this, you will automatically increase the amount of ownership people have in what you are doing. Loving your city requires community wide participation, so building that mindset from the beginning is crucial.

As you grow, so will your needs, but so will the pool of potential donors. Some people will not be able to give much, but they want to help. Others, having caught the vision for what you are doing, may well be able to give a great deal. No matter the size of the gift, you will never get anything if you don't ask. That's what most of us have a hard time with. It is not that we don't believe in our cause, it's that we don't want to feel slimy and asking for money often makes us feel that way. The thing is, when people buy into what you are doing, they are often more than happy to help. So let's look at two keys to successful fundraising.

Two Keys to Successful Fundraising

Most fundraising fails either because the person doing the fundraising is poor at communicating their purpose, or the vision and plan to achieve that purpose is not very compelling to the people who are hearing the message. Conversely, most successful fundraisers can clearly articulate a vision that inspires others and can provide a roadmap showing why they have been successful and how they will continue to be successful in the future.

Most of us believe we have a clear vision for what our ministry or organization does, but the proof is in being able to articulate that purpose clearly and concisely to others. It's the famous elevator pitch—can you make a compelling case for what you do in 30 seconds to a minute? A few years ago, a friend and I attempted to raise capital from Venture Capitalists for a project. We thought we had a great idea that would change the world, but when we attempted to communicate that vision in front of others, we quickly realized we had a problem. There were major gaps in our communication and strategy that had to be addressed before someone could quickly understand what we were trying to accomplish. The same is true for you as you look to build your community engagement initiative.

Over the years at Love Modesto and Love Our Cities, we have learned two very important lessons that have helped us acquire donors.

Lesson #1: People won't get behind something they don't understand.

At Love Our Cities, we boiled down our value proposition to one phrase, "We help leaders run city-wide volunteer days." It's the first thing you see on our website. Remember, it's our core value add. If there is one thing that people immediately get, it's that. From there we can tell the story of why it's important and how we are making an impact in cities all over the country.

This simple statement has been a launching point for us to quickly identify with our audience. If they (if you!) resonate with our value proposition, then we have an instant connection to build on and we can take the next step. If the response to our value proposition isn't positive, then the reality is that there is probably not a good match and we can both move on and not waste each other's time.

This kind of simplicity is also at the heart of our branding. The "Love _____" brand is both simple and transparent. It is not a value proposition in the same way, but it has an instant emotional connection.

As you start thinking seriously about what you are trying to achieve, ask yourself: Can we clearly communicate our value proposition in one phrase? As a leadership team, you need to spend time working on this statement. When you have something that you think really does the job, ask yourselves "Who can we present to that will give us honest feedback to help refine our communications?

When you can clearly present a compelling reason for people to give, you will notice that more people will be willing to contribute to you. You will also find that it is much easier to ask because you won't feel like you don't know what to say or how to say it. This is an investment in time and effort that will literally pay off.

Lesson #2: Funders are not just check books, they're co-conspirators.

Being clear in communicating who you are and what you are about is only the first step. In order for people to support you, they have to believe in what you are doing and why. When you fundraise, you are not only asking people to back you financially, but you are asking them to partner with you in your mission. If they are not aligned with you philosophically and emotionally, they probably aren't going to be a donor. When you are doing what we do, creating a way to help your city by championing others, this is even more crucial.

We have multiple funding streams at Love Modesto and Love Our Cities (more on that in the next section), and each one requires a different approach in our communications. When we talk to our church partners (or possible church partners), we focus on being an extension of their local outreach and helping them to connect with their community. When we approach business sponsors, we focus on the work we do in the community and how they can benefit from aligning themselves with our brand. Each group has a different set of needs and value propositions that matter to them (whether they have an official statement or not), and each need to be addressed uniquely.

When you show donors the value-add you are providing them by working together, you not only are able to raise funds, but you gain co-conspirators. They become invested in you and your success. Co-conspirators are crucial because they do more than simply provide money. They provide connections. When you invest in something you are likely to talk about it. When you sign up co-conspirators, chances are they know people and opportunities that you don't. They will help you to expand your network and as it grows, so will your collective wisdom and access to opportunities both for service as well as for other donors.

Our network has introduced us to other sponsors, grants, and opportunities to work in our community that we never would have had access to without them. Some of these come from partner organizations, some from volunteers and our board members, but others come from financial partners that are vested in our success.

Once you have your core communication statement nailed, you need to think about how you are approaching different prospective funders and positioning your messaging to align with their goals. How does what you communicate invite them to partner with you? Let me be clear, I am not advocating being a chameleon or saying whatever you think a big donor will want to hear. That is exactly the kind of thing that makes people not want to ask for (or give) money. Your core message can't change. What does change is the connection point for alignment with you. The goal is not to get as much money as you can from whomever you can, it is to find legitimate partners who will invest in what you are doing. That requires honesty that is presented in the way your partners think, not slick marketing gimmicks.

The more we have focused on these two lessons, the more we've found success in our fundraising efforts. These lessons have and continue to help us grow and mature and they can do the same for you.

Should You Become Your Own Nonprofit?

Way back in chapter three, Jeff talked about going full time and becoming a nonprofit separate from the church where Love Modesto started. It was a strategic decision based on how things were developing both in Modesto itself and as we began to help more and more communities, many of which didn't have a direct connection with Modesto or Big Valley Grace. It is unlikely that you will face that kind of situation. Like April in Madera, however, you may get to the point where you do need to start thinking about going full-time yourself.

When Love Modesto started, Jeff basically had three options:

Stay on staff at the church he was working for

Find another existing nonprofit for Love Modesto to fit under (and for Jeff to work for)

Start a nonprofit

Each option has advantages and disadvantages. For example, option 1: pro—stable income and support; con—limited broad-based community support and a regular need to show why it fits. Both the pros and the cons are important to wrestle with. In the end we are really glad we went with option three. It has provided many benefits for us in the long run (even though we have had some trying times). It has allowed us to keep laser focused on our mission, adapt when we have needed to, and it has provided us with the ability to pursue diverse funding streams which can be very important.

Not everyone needs to start their own nonprofit. Some cities are small, and it simply doesn't require that kind of time (though you may be surprised). Certainly, for the first year or so you won't need to. There are ways to do fundraising through the main donor organizations that you are working through. We can't give you a hard and fast rule about whether to or when to become your own nonprofit. We can tell you that in our experience, at some point you will probably need to do so. It may sound overwhelming, but we have helped lots of cities do just that.

So why are we bringing this question up here? Because in many ways it is tied to funding what you are doing. If you and your leadership team are entirely volunteers and there is little overhead, then your fundraising needs can be kept smaller. But once you head through the paradigm shift of loving your city year-round, things will change, there is simply no way around it. You can probably still stay small (we have, and we are both a local and a nationwide organization) but there is only so much that can be done without someone who is working at this full-time, and that means someone needs to be paid.

When you have an employee, even if there is just one and it's you, then expenses go up. There's a salary (even if it's small), taxes, office supplies and phones, and, well, you get the picture. Is it worth it? Couldn't the expenses of staff and overhead just go directly to the things that you are trying to accomplish with less money? Well, yes, it is worth it. Maybe you could save money, but maybe not. And saving money isn't the only criteria you should be using to evaluate this decision. Remembering our belief that bigger is not necessarily better, the questions you need to ask at this stage involve more than saving money. The better question is whether being a nonprofit will allow you to use the money you do have access to in a more efficient manner.

It will require more money to have a person on staff, but that person will be able to help deploy the funds that you do have in ways that will allow them to have maximum impact. It can allow for the development of a greater network of people who are invested in what you do, offer new opportunities for you to engage in community service, increase the numbers of volunteers, even find new donors. You get the picture, right? Becoming your own nonprofit is not a small step. It will require more fundraising, and it may not be the right step for you right now, but it does have significant advantages.

The Importance of Multiple Fundraising Channels

On July 26th, 1956, Egyptian President Gamal Abdel Nasser gave a speech declaring that the Suez Canal was being nationalized. At the same moment, Egyptian forces raided and took control of the important trade route. While in many ways it was disastrous for the British politically, one of the biggest blows was what it meant for them economically. At that time, 2/3 of England's oil was being imported via the canal. With the canal now closed to their ships, their oil dependent country was suddenly brought to its knees.

Even if you understand and agree with every last thing that we have talked about so far in this chapter, when it comes to fundraising, there is no question that most of us would be perfectly content to rely on one revenue stream. After all, if you could get your fundraising done in one fell swoop then you could get on to the good stuff, right? The inherent risk, however, is that if your one stream suddenly disappears overnight, you will find yourself in the same position as the British in 1956—on the brink of crises. What happens when that single church who has been underwriting everything you do decides to reallocate all of their funds or when your angel investor dies and leaves no ongoing provision for your organization? While multiple revenue streams can take more effort, the diversity provides stability. With multiple streams, a major fluctuation in one stream becomes painful, but rarely so detrimental that there is a crisis.

No two cities we work with have exactly the same fundraising channels, but we have found some general rules of thumb from our experience both locally with Love Modesto and Nationally with Love Our Cities. Our multichannel strategy has helped us to create a very stable financial picture. Our 5 main channels are:

1. Church Partners
2. Business/ Event Sponsors
3. Fundraisers
4. Individual supporters
5. Grants

Church Partners

While Church Partners are no longer our biggest category, they are our backbone, both financially and spiritually. We truly believe that we are an extension of the local church, and we approach churches with the idea of being a key resource for their local missions outreach. We help provide volunteer opportunities throughout the year and we are a neutral convener that the church can work through to address larger needs in our community with government, business, and nonprofits. Many churches have found that they can make their mission budgets go much farther by partnering with us than they ever could have done on their own.

At our annual Love Modesto volunteer day, we group all our Church Partners together on one banner and hang it on stage so the community can see that the event is backed by the church community and the church community is working together. It is a visual expression of church unity in our community.

Each church supports us at a different level, depending on the size of church and availability of resources. Some of our partner cities approach churches more systematically, others ask churches simply to be an Event or Project Sponsor. There are multiple models, but church partners are always a main pillar in our funding strategy and as we have talked about repeatedly, they will be your first stop as you develop your city engagement initiative.

Business/Event Sponsors

Our Love Modesto city wide volunteer day really is the backbone of our organization and is also the biggest piece of our fundraising efforts. As a reminder, in 2019 in Modesto alone, we had over 7,250 participants spanning 110 projects, including a morning rally prior to the day that drew over 5,000 people. When you think of the impact across over 90 cities and 40,000 volunteers in one year alone, then adding up all the years we have been doing these events, that's a lot of impact. The city-wide volunteer day is not only the flywheel that brings the community together to do great things for the city, but also the single largest means of raising funds for our ongoing operations.

The event provides various sponsorship opportunities from all sectors in the city. We have several different sponsorship levels available in addition to our projects. Businesses, churches, and nonprofits all are willing to support a project that they care about. Some businesses have also partnered with us on a longer-term basis, though most of them started as event sponsors. In the chart above you will notice a smaller slice for the comfort kits that we talked about in chapter 11. While these funds are highly targeted (and often include items not just funds) they are a part of an event.

The city-wide volunteer day not only produces event sponsors, but it has become a huge catalytic event that builds momentum and has led to other funding opportunities. In Modesto, our volunteer day has led to our involvement in many other initiatives and access to funding including grants. One of our city partners recently received a $200,000 grant to help fight gang violence in their community. Their board attributed success in receiving the grant, in part, to the visibility from the city-wide volunteer day and how it made them known in the community.

While fundraising isn't the reason we do any of these events, the city-wide volunteer day in particular functions on two levels at once, providing both a means for us to champion the good things that people in our community are doing and offering a tremendous opportunity to cover our operating expenses for the year.

Fundraisers

While it is technically another event, every fall we have an annual golf tournament. The difference between this event and literally every other one we do is that it is the only event we do that is strictly a fundraiser. Every other event is geared towards a specific initiative or cause (neighborhoods, schools, foster kids, etc.). Our annual Golf Tournament is our way of raising awareness of our organization and a chance to deepen relationships with business owners.

It doesn't have to be a golf tournament, but we have found that it works well for us. Other cities have done galas or things like that, the point is an event where people come to have a good time and they know that they are going to be asked for a donation. It takes quite a bit of effort to put on an event like this, but with a good volunteer team and a couple of years under our belt, we've found that the process has become easier, the sponsors are more eager to respond, and the day becomes a lot of fun. We still have room to grow in this arena ourselves, but it has become a significant part of our yearly fundraising.

Individuals

Over the years as people have caught the vision for what we are trying to do, we have received donations from individuals. Sometimes they are one-time gifts and sometimes they are monthly partners. Together these donations from individuals make up over 10% of our operating revenue. We make it a point to make the ability to donate both easy to see and easy to accomplish on our website. It is easy to overlook the importance of small donors, but they are crucial to our ongoing ability to love our city, and they will be for you as well.

One aspect about individual donations that you may not have considered, and frankly it is another reason why you shouldn't be afraid to ask for donations. Some people simply can't get out to help with the projects either on the city-wide volunteer day or perhaps even throughout the year. Perhaps they are out of town on the day of the event or they have physical limitations, but they want to be a part of what you are doing. Don't keep that opportunity from them.

Grants

I mentioned grants briefly above and I am not going to say too much more. Grants are a bit tricky and you are not likely to run into them in the first few years as you build up your organization. Grants are generally for a specific timeframe and/or purpose. They may or may not be recurring, so they are hard to budget around, especially if they are for a one-time project. They can, however, be of great use in certain situations, including underwriting a staff person to administer a specific project. Over time and as you establish yourself, they may come into play.

Concluding Thoughts on Funding

The reality is, just like the needs of any given city, each situation is unique. Resources will look differently for you than us in Modesto. We've adopted some strategies from other organizations that have been home runs for us. Some others have failed, and others we weren't allowed to do because of state regulations. It's not like any of the things we have outlined above have produced millions of dollars, but they have worked well, provided us some stability and diversity, and have allowed us to do the work that we love with some great funding partners.

It is unlikely that fundraising will ever be the number one fun thing on your to-do list (if it is, we need to talk), but it is a vital part of what you will be doing as you seek to develop a city engagement initiative in your city. Here's the carrot: if you want to do this, you can—we have seen it happen over and over again. And just like the nuts and bolts of running the volunteer day and getting you up and running, part of what we do every day is help people like you make this work. We have a process, and we can help you make it happen.

Afterword:

Your City Spotlight

You made it. You have heard our story; heard why we do what we do and how we do it. We have tried to make it short (because we want to get in there and get going just like you do) and practical (because if it's just a lot of blah, blah, blah then we both know that little will come of it). We also gave you glimpses of some of the cities that we have partnered with over the years. Cities with people just like you who decided that they were going to make things different in their cities. We hope that we have inspired you to take a risk and start loving your city in a whole new way.

So here's your task. We want you to write your own city spotlight. Tell us about your city. Where are you from? What do you love about your city? What are the needs that you see? What do you dream for your city? Remember, the good news—as overwhelming as the challenges seem, chances are you don't have to start anything new. You have to show compassion with a humble spirit. You have to build trust and relationships in your city and get people together.

Reread the city spotlights and write your own. Then send it to us. Drop us an email at jeff@loveourcities.org and eric@loveourcities.org. We really do want to hear from you. Who knows, maybe someday there will be a volume 2 and your name and your city will be there. We would love to partner with you to create your own city-wide volunteer day of your very own. This is what we do. So write your own spotlight, send it to us, and spend some time at www.loveourcities.org to see how we can walk with you as you love your city.

(Dream Big!)

Acknowledgments

We would like to thank our families—our wives and kids who have supported us as we worked to fulfill the dream of creating this book. Eric Swanson, Kevin Palau, Marvin Jacobo, Scott Miller, Gordon Rumble and others encouraged us to write this in the first place. Kevin O'Brien worked from the very beginning helping us structure the book, turned a couple of days of interviews into an actual manuscript, worked on editing, and then publication. Dan Balow who worked through the publication process. Founding board members, John Evans and Chuck Bryant were instrumental in this effort. And finally, Terry Whalin and Morgan James who agreed to publish it.

Obviously, there are a whole lot more that we could and should name. We especially want to thank all the cities, leaders and volunteers who have partnered with us over the years. This book only exists because of you.

Jeff and Eric

About the Authors

Jeff Pishney, CEO and Founder Love Modesto (now Love Stanislaus County) and Love Our Cities

Jeff grew up in Iowa, went to college and graduate school in Virginia and has lived in Modesto, CA since 1995. Prior to being executive director, Jeff was a pastor for almost 20 years at Big Valley Grace Community Church. Jeff's vision for his community began to form as College Pastor and grew when he became Outreach Pastor. During that period Love Modesto  began. Officially becoming a nonprofit organization in 2014, Love Modesto's community-wide volunteer days have spawned a movement reaching over 100 cities, and over 250,000 volunteers since beginning in 2009. Jeff recognizes that more sustainable solutions are needed beyond volunteer days in order to see our cities thrive. Through his leadership, Love Modesto and Love Our Cities have become hubs for community engagement in cities across the United States. His efforts have evolved to championing ongoing volunteerism, collaboration among leaders and initiating the local efforts of Love Our Neighbors, Love Our Schools, Love Our Kids, and Love Our Seniors.

Jeff and his wife, Karen, have been married for 18 years and have three children. Besides loving his family, Jeff is involved at his children's activities, passionate about social justice issues and cheering on his Iowa Hawkeyes.

Eric Jung, Director of Policy Titan Solar Power and Love Our Cities Board Member

Eric Jung is a founding board member of Love Our Cities and was the first employee hired to help Jeff scale the move-ment. As City Engagement Director, Eric solid-ified the infrastructure so that Love Our Cities could support hundreds of cities to run city-wide volunteer days. Locally, Eric helped create contractual relationships with city, county, and other nonprofit organizations to provide long term funding for Love Our Neighbors, Love Our Schools, and Love Our Kids. During the onset of COVID, Eric coordinated efforts across all sectors of our county to create, overnight, an online clearinghouse for people needing food deliv-ered to them and people wanting to volunteer.

Eric is a California native, from the Bay Area to San Diego and now the Central Valley. With an undergraduate degree in Business Finance and a Seminary Degree in Theology and Leadership, Eric is passionate about the Church reclaiming its role and value in the community. Eric and his wife, Kara, have five children ranging from 3-13 years in age. Eric loves Bay Area sports teams and date nights with his wife on the golf course. While still a board member for Love Our Cities, Eric currently is the Director of Policy for Titan Solar Power, the largest privately held residen-tial solar installer in the US.

A free ebook edition
is available with the
purchase of this book.

To claim your free ebook edition:

1. Visit MorganJamesBOGO.com
2. Sign your name CLEARLY in the space
3. Complete the form and submit a photo of the entire copyright page
4. You or your friend can download the ebook to your preferred device

A **FREE** ebook edition is available for you
or a friend with the purchase of this print book.

CLEARLY SIGN YOUR NAME ABOVE

Instructions to claim your free ebook edition:
1. Visit MorganJamesBOGO.com
2. Sign your name CLEARLY in the space above
3. Complete the form and submit a photo
   of this entire page
4. You or your friend can download the ebook
   to your preferred device

Print & Digital Together Forever.

Snap a photo

Free ebook

Read anywhere